The Wisdom of Jesus

The Wisdom Jesus

*Transforming Heart and Mind—
a New Perspective on Christ
and His Message*

Cynthia
Bourgeault

Shambhala
Boston & London
2008

Shambhala Publications, Inc.
Horticultural Hall
300 Massachusetts Avenue
Boston, Massachusetts 02115
www.shambhala.com

9 8 7 6 5 4 3 2 1
First Edition
Printed in the United States of America

⊗ This edition is printed on acid-free paper that meets
the American National Standards Institute z39.48 Standard.
Distributed in the United States by Random House, Inc.,
and in Canada by Random House of Canada Ltd.

Library of Congress Cataloging-in-Publication Data
Bourgeault, Cynthia.
The wisdom Jesus: transforming heart and mind: a new perspective
on Christ and his message/Cynthia Bourgeault.—1st ed.
p. cm.
Includes bibliographical references and index.
ISBN 978-1-59030-580-5 (pbk.: alk. paper)
1. Jesus Christ. I. Title.
BT304.9.B68 2008
232—DC22
2007044952

To Gregg Anderson
Thank you for thirty years of holding the space.

Contents

PART THREE

Christian Wisdom Practices

Acknowledgments

My heartfelt gratitude to Nancy Smith, managing editor at Sounds True, who first invited me to shape several years' worth of class notes and lectures into a CD teaching series called *Encountering the Wisdom Jesus*. We recorded the material in an intense three-day marathon in November 2004, and the six-CD teaching set made its debut in April 2005. The present book is an adaptation and expansion of that original product (if you prefer your learning in audio form, the series is still easily available at www.soundstrue.com). Nancy's skill, sensitivity, and vision are an inseparable part of this work, and she is its official midwife. As always, I am grateful to the entire Sounds True team for their exemplary professionalism, helpfulness, and graciousness.

To my dear friend Robert Pynn, dean emeritus of the Anglican Cathedral in Calgary, Alberta, who urged me to adapt the material to book form and took the decisive step in making it happen: arranging for it to be transcribed into written form. To Ellen Lea, who patiently converted twelve hours of teaching into 108 single-spaced manuscript pages, virtually flawlessly. I am not only grateful, but amazed!

To Dave O'Neal, my editor at Shambhala Publications, who took the material from transcript to manuscript with a finely tuned discernment and steady encouragement.

To Rami Shapiro and Lynn Bauman, longtime friends and colleagues, who read the manuscript closely and offered helpful comments and clarifications. To Ed Bastian and my fellow faculty members at the Spiritual Paths Institute, who have helped me to reintroduce the Wisdom Jesus to a wider interspiritual audience. To Ken Wilber for his brilliant paradigms, and to Sherif Baba Chatalkaya for his boundless heart.

To my many students over the years, particularly in the Aspen Wisdom School, who have helped me work through every bit of this material. And to my faithful friends in the Contemplative Society in Victoria, British Columbia, whose prayers and financial support made it possible to bring the project to completion.

Finally, I would like to acknowledge in a special way The Rt. Rev. Robert J. O'Neill, my bishop here in Colorado, whose steadfast support during these past five years has been a crucial ingredient in the emergence of my own writer's voice. In these times of spiritual ferment, when one hardly knows whether one is a midwife or a hospice worker to the traditional forms of institutional Christianity, Bishop O'Neill has led the way with clarity, compassion, and imagination. He renews my faith that Christianity will emerge from this time of winnowing with a deeper and more authentic commitment to the path of its risen Master.

PART ONE

The Teachings of Jesus

I

Jesus as a Recognition Event

If you are searching,
You must not stop until you find.
When you find, however,
You will become troubled.
Your confusion will give way to wonder.
In wonder you will reign over all things.
Your sovereignty will be your rest.[1]

T HE WORDS ABOVE are from the Gospel of Thomas, recovered in 1945 amid the Nag Hammadi scrolls in the Egyptian desert and now largely accepted as an authentic teaching of Jesus. The quotation in this version is probably longer than you're familiar with from the Bible; the other gospels stop with "seek and you shall find." But here Jesus lays out several additional steps to tell us what the search is *really* like. Seeking leads to finding, yes, but the result of that finding is often to plunge you into confusion and disorientation as the new information rattles the cage of your old paradigm. Only gradually, as you can make room for what this gospel calls "wonder," does a new

universe begin to knit itself together around you, and you come
to rest on a new foundation. Until the next go-round, that is.

Thomas's words are timely because in this book we'll be
embarking on an exploration of some rich spiritual territory,
which may be very challenging precisely because it's so near at
hand. We will be attempting a new take on Jesus, a new look at
him as a master in an ancient spiritual tradition which I'll call
wisdom. This is difficult precisely because most of us think we
know something about this Jesus already. We don't all agree on
what we know, of course. But if you've grown up Christian, you
at least know the general gist of the story—that he was the only
Son of God, that he came to this world on a mission of teaching
and healing, that he was crucified, died for our sins, rose again,
ascended into heaven, and now asks us to believe. Believe what?
Well, believe all the things I've just said.

Perhaps the most deadening aspect of our Christianity as
we're used to it—aside from the fact that it really is a kind of cultural backdrop, the filter through which we look at everything
else—is that we live it with twenty-twenty hindsight. We know
the story. We know how the plot comes out. We know who the
winners are, what the winning team is all about. We celebrate
this story again and again, in our grand festivals at Christmas
and Easter, and in smaller segments throughout the year. If you
go to the Catholic or Episcopal Church, every Sunday you'll
recite the story in the form of the Nicene Creed: "We believe in
one God, the Father Almighty, Creator of heaven and earth, of
all that is, seen and unseen. We believe in one Lord, Jesus Christ,
the only Son of God, eternally begotten of the Father, God from
God, Light from Light, true God from true God; begotten, not
made, one in being with the Father, through whom all things
were made," and so on. Christians have been doing this since
the fourth century. It's the primary way that we approach our
teacher, through what we believe about him. And if you're of
the fundamentalist or evangelical persuasion, you'll know that
the whole story is there in scripture. The Bible contains the
complete and divinely authorized biography of Jesus and furnishes the complete guide to what you should do to become

his disciple. Everything needed for your personal salvation is right there. But what I'm about to suggest as the starting point for our exploration is that all this knowing about Jesus actually gets in the way. Living our Christianity with twenty-twenty hindsight lands us in trouble in at least two ways. First of all, it lulls us into a false sense of security: that we're the winning team, that as Christians we'd recognize and know Jesus when he showed up. But even more problematically, this twenty-twenty hindsight takes away from us the key tool that we need to find and live the path today, to connect with this person that we seem to know so much about. This tool is our own power of inner recognition, and I will have much to say about it shortly.

But of course we may be in a window of opportunity just here. We're living in an era in which the Christian monolith is breaking down. Some would say it's broken down already. Mainstream Christianity is steadily losing ground (and membership). Across the board—between denominations and within them as well—forward movement seems to have slowed to a halt in the violent polarization between left wing and right wing, between liberal and fundamentalist takes on reality. You see Christian communities tearing themselves to pieces over issues such as the blessing of homosexual unions, or women's ordination, or abortion rights, while the gospel call to tend the poor and speak truth to power goes increasingly unheeded. There's so much anguish and struggle within an institution which even fifty years ago was virtually (or virtuously) synonymous with the decent and proper conduct of society. And at the same time there's a lot of new information out there—even gospels we didn't really know about before, like the Gospel of Thomas, discovered among the so-called gnostic gospels, the cache of ancient Christian texts found at Nag Hammadi in 1945. And there's a lot of speculation and revisioning emerging from these recent discoveries, some parts of it very solid and others downright flaky.

In other words, we're living in an era right now which some would call a major paradigm shift, where there's an opportunity as perhaps there hasn't been before to really open up the core questions again and ask, "What is it that we mean by 'Christian-ity'? What is this filter that we're looking through? Who is this Master that we profess and confess in our life as we call ourselves Christian?"

The angle of approach I will be using throughout this book is to see Jesus first and foremost as a wisdom teacher, a person who (for the moment setting aside the whole issue of his divine par-entage) clearly emerges out of and works within an ancient tra-dition called "wisdom," sometimes known as *sophia perennis*, which is in fact at the headwaters of all the great religious tradi-tions of the world today. It's concerned with the transformation of the whole human being. Transformation from what to what? Well, for a starter, from our animal instincts and egocentricity into love and compassion; from a judgmental and dualistic worldview into a nondual acceptingness. This was the message that Jesus, apparently out of nowhere, came preaching and teaching, a message that was radical in its own time and remains equally radical today. I'm mindful here of one of my favorite quotes, attributed to the British writer G. K. Chesterton, who reportedly said, "Christianity isn't a failure; it just hasn't been tried yet." In this great cultural monolith that we call Christian-ity, which has guided the course of Western history for more than two thousand years, have we really yet unlocked the power to deeply understand and follow this Jesus along the radical path he is calling us to?

I realize that we'll be traversing some volatile territory here. Some of material I'll be presenting will challenge your assump-tions, even your most cherished assumptions. It's a new way of putting the pieces together. As we embark together on this journey into the unknown, it is important for you to trust your guide. So I want to begin by saying a little bit about who I am and how I've come to where I am on this path.

The official version is that I am an Episcopal priest, a writer, and a retreat leader. I am also a woman, and that means that some of my recent history in the church has been filled with struggle and contentiousness. I wasn't in the very first group of women ordained in the Episcopal Church (which happened unofficially in 1974 and officially in 1977), but I am almost certainly among the first few hundred, since my ordination in 1979 came only two years after the church had committed itself to this path. In some other denominations it's still unthinkable. So I've come through a time of turmoil and testing the waters, as my Church moved through a great consciousness shift. I'm a contemplative, by which I mean, in the Christian tradition, that my spiritual practice is grounded in a regular practice of meditation, silent prayer, and quiet scriptural reading. I've worked closely with Father Thomas Keating at St. Benedict's Monastery in Colorado on the practice of Centering Prayer. It's been my meditation practice for more than two decades, and it's through this, and that other ancient monastic discipline called *lectio divina* (sacred reading) that I've come to most of what I know from the inside about our Christian walk and tradition.

Since the mid-1980s I've also been a serious student of the worldwide wisdom tradition. I've participated in the Gurdjieff work, in Sufism (the mystical arm of Islam), and a bit in Vedanta and Kabbalah studies, and I'm one of the core faculty members in a wonderful new organization called the Spiritual Paths Institute in Santa Barbara, California, which brings together teachers from all the great faith traditions to share insights and contemplative practice. From this wider immersion I've been reaffirmed in my sense that Jesus came first and foremost as a teacher of the path of inner transformation. That doesn't take away the Jesus you may be more familiar with—the Son of God, the second person of the Trinity—but it does add a renewed emphasis on paying attention to what he actually taught and seeing how we can begin to walk it authentically from the inside. It also suggests that he did not really come out of nowhere, but rather that he belongs to a stream of living wisdom that has been flowing through the human condition for at least five thousand years.

That's the external story of who I am, the credentials and background that I bring to this undertaking. But the real story is more inward, as such stories always are. I'm first and foremost a seeker, and in my own journey, the most important thing I had to learn was not what to seek, but *how* to seek. I grew up in eastern Pennsylvania in the 1950s, raised as a Christian Scientist officially, but I was sent to a Quaker school for my early education. Now these two streams of religious experience are pretty much polar opposites. Christian Science is a highly mental religion, teaching and exhorting one to apply the mind around universal metaphysical principles so as to be able to replicate what Jesus did in his healing. And Quakerism, particularly in these deep, silent meetings for worship that were part of my school life from the time I was in kindergarten till the end of fourth grade, was simply an unprogrammed, unmediated experience of being thrown off the diving-board into the direct presence of God. Once a week on Thursday mornings all sixty-five of us students, ages five through twelve, were marched into the cavernous, colonial meeting house next door to the school and simply asked to sit silently in the presence of God. If the spirit moved us, we were permitted to rise and offer a short prayer, Bible verse, or reflection. No one ever gave us instructions on how to do it; it was simply assumed that once you entered the silence, you'd instinctively know what to do next, like a duckling taking to water.

For much of my childhood, then, I grew up with these two very conflicting streams of religious experience which I couldn't reconcile. One day when I was about twelve years old they got reconciled in a way that was so completely unexpected that I've never forgotten it. It was probably the foundational moment of my own religious journey. Next door to us lived Dan and Betsy Hoopes, and their four kids, who were my playmates. The fall of my sixth-grade year, Dan Hoopes's kidneys began to fail— gradually at first, then with alarming rapidity. He was taken by ambulance to the hospital and moved directly into intensive care. Soon afterward my parents called my brother and me into their bedroom and sadly told us that Dan was dying. As a young Christian Scientist, this created a crisis for me, because I had been working hard with my Christian Science, as best as I could understand it as a child, trying to do the proper "knowing" that Dan's illness was just simply an unreal claim of mortal mind and that all would be well. But now he was dying anyway, and it all seemed futile. I slipped outside to ponder the situation, taking refuge in the park across the street from my house. It was a snowy evening, late November or early December. I raged at God. "What's wrong here? Is there something wrong with me or with you? Why isn't this working? How can this happen?"

All of a sudden I felt myself suffused in golden light, very much like I'd experienced in those Quaker meetings, and I heard a voice distinctly saying, "Shhh. Dan will die . . . and all will be well." While I certainly couldn't understand the message itself, I understood that warm, golden light and somehow relaxed and rested. I discovered in that moment that there was something in me that knew. It didn't know *what* it knew, exactly, but it knew *that* it knew. Deeper than all the precepts that had been drilled into me in my childhood religious training, it simply recognized the voice of truth when it heard it and let go into its presence.

Which brings me back to the topic I started with: living our Christianity with twenty-twenty hindsight. The real problem is that when we do that, we get lulled into "ordinary knowledge" (as the contemporary spiritual teacher A. H. Almaas calls it²) and nothing spiritually real can happen there. When we approach the story with the attitude, "I've heard that already, I know what that means," we fall asleep rather than allowing ourselves to be shocked awake. As in the Gospel of Thomas, it's merely the "seek and you shall find" part without the confusion, wonder, and reorientation—and also, without the "sovereignty." For all such spiritual sleepwalking bypasses that crucial first step, that moment when the heart has to find its way not through external conditioning but through a raw immediacy of presence. Only there—in "the cave of the heart," as the mystics are fond of calling it—does a person come in contact with his or her own direct knowingness. And only out of this direct knowingness is sovereignty born, one's own inner authority.

Let's take a wild leap, then, and imagine ourselves beside the shores of the Sea of Galilee two thousand years ago, with absolutely no idea of how the story will turn out. A new teacher has appeared on the scene, and no one knows exactly where he came up with what he's teaching. People say that he used to be a devotee of John the Baptist, but he's preaching a very different message from John—and certainly from what the rabbis are up to in the synagogues—and people are divided about him. Some say, "This is the most amazing, strange, wild, true stuff I've ever heard." And others say, "But wait a minute! My rabbi says that he's breaking the law, he's healing on the Sabbath, he's disrespecting the law and the prophets. You'd better beware of him. He's dangerous." Now say that both of these opinions are jostling in your head as you approach the Sea of Galilee. How do you know, when you stand before this man for the very first time, whether he's trustworthy or not? Whether you will give your heart to him or keep your distance? He isn't wearing a crown of gold (or a crown of thorns either). He looks like anybody else, except for the intense light in his eyes beckoning you forward. And as you step into that circle of light, what are you thrust back upon? Your own naked knowingness. You are face to face with the same thing I came face to face with that evening in the park.

"Who do you say I am?" Jesus asks repeatedly throughout the gospels. Which really means, "Who or what in you recognizes me?" It is the crucial question.

One of my own most important mentors along the path is Father Bruno Barnhart, who for many years was prior of the Benedictine Camaldolese Monastery in Big Sur, California. He still lives there as a hermit and a writer and is widely admired for his mystical brilliance. He was the first person who really put the pieces together for me: that the key ingredient I've been talking about is really *recognition energy*. It's the capacity to ground-truth a spiritual experience in your own being. The gospels are built on it—and so was the early church—as the powerful liberation energy of the Christ event spills over and travels forward, moving from recognition to recognition. In his wonderful book *Second Simplicity,* Father Bruno explains what he means:

> As we accompany Jesus through the gospels we are present at one dramatic meeting after another. "One person after another experiences a mysterious power in Jesus

that from this moment changes the course of his or her
life. If we are fully present at the moment when we read
such a narrative, we ourselves experience the liberating
power of this awakening. Examples come quickly to
mind: The two disciples in John's first chapter: "Rabbi,
where do you dwell?" "Come and see." Then quickly
in that same Johannine narrative, Peter and Nathaniel
experience the awakening of meeting Jesus. In the synoptic gospels we may recall the reaction to Jesus of the
blind man alongside the road to Jericho, of the father
of the paralytic boy, of the centurion whose servant was
sick, of the thief on the cross alongside Jesus, of the centurion present at Jesus' death. Time after time we feel
the break-through of life, the wave-front of wonder.[3]

"Well, of course," you may say, "it would be easy to recognize Jesus. He's the one that rose from the dead." And you
may assume that these early Christian disciples flocked to Jesus
because of the resurrection. I once asked a group of people in a
church I served, "Would it make any difference for you if the resurrection hadn't happened, if Jesus hadn't risen from the dead?"
I admit it was a trick question, and I got exactly the response
I expected: theological diatribes based on the Nicene Creed.
Of *course* it would make a difference: because the resurrection
proves that Jesus is the only Son of God, that there is none other
like him, that in and through him God has reconciled heaven
and earth and laid the foundations of the New Creation, that
this is the pivotal moment in salvation history   on and on like
that. But the point being missed—and it's really a key point—
is that for these first disciples, the ones who first listened and
said "yes" to Jesus, *the outcome was as yet unknown*. Both crucifixion and resurrection lay ahead. How would they know that
this teacher whose being was pouring into them, sometimes in
spite of themselves, in the midst of the crosscurrents in their
hearts, would all too soon be crucified, die, and rise again? It all
lay up ahead. What caused them to say "yes" to Jesus? It must
have been very different from what now, twenty centuries later,

is our normal understanding of the situation. We may say "yes" to Jesus because we know now that he is the Son of God, that he died and rose again, and that in union with him we hope to do likewise. They didn't know this. What said "yes"?

I'd like to explore this question more deeply by looking at one of the most interesting and significant people who said "yes": the Samaritan woman at the well, whose story we read in the fourth chapter of the Gospel of John. To fill in a bit of the background, Samaria and Judea were adjacent Israelite kingdoms. While Samaritans and Jews were both Semitic people, descendants of the original twelve tribes of Israel, they had been at odds with each other for centuries, and Jews normally didn't speak to Samaritans. Certainly Jewish men didn't speak to Samaritan women. So there's something very striking and odd in the configuration of this story to begin with. At high noon, Jesus draws up to a well in Samaria (in order to travel from Galilee to Jerusalem one has to cross Samaria) and asks a woman drawing water there for a drink of water. Here is the dialogue that ensues, found in John 4:6–15:

> Jesus, tired out by his journey, was sitting by the well. It was about noon. A Samaritan woman came to draw water, and Jesus said to her, "Give me a drink." (His disciples had gone to the city to buy food.) The Samaritan woman said to him, "How is it that you, a Jew, ask a drink of me, a woman of Samaria?" (Jews do not share things in common with Samaritans.) Jesus answered her, "If you knew the gift of God, and who it is that is saying to you, 'Give me a drink,' you would have asked him, and he would have given you living water." The woman said to him, "Sir, you have no bucket, and the well is deep. Where do you get that living water? Are you greater than our ancestor Jacob, who gave us the well, and with his sons and flocks drank from it?" Jesus said to her, "Everyone who drinks of this water will be thirsty again, but those who drink of the water that I will give them will never be thirsty. The water that I will

give will become in them a spring of water gushing up
to eternal life." The woman said to him, "Sir, give me
this water, so that I may never be thirsty, or have to keep
coming here to draw water."[4]

It is an interesting and powerful encounter. When I listen
closely, the first thing I hear is a sort of mutual boldness. Clearly Jesus sees something in this woman from the start, for him
even to begin to address her. And far from being intimidated,
she returns his serves beautifully. When he talks about water she
challenges him, but when he ups the ante and moves from literal
water (that water down in that well that you haul with a bucket)
to living water, she goes right along with him. And when he says,
"With the water that I give you, you will never thirst again," she
catches his meaning exactly; she makes the leap right along with
him. It's a fascinating exchange. There is a heart-to-heart connection and a heart-to-heart inner seeing. He sees who she is;
she sees who he is. And in the light of that mutual recognition
they keep on empowering each other and drawing each other
along to a greater self-disclosure, until finally, a few lines later,
Jesus says to her, "The hour is coming and is even now here
when the true worshipers will worship the Father in spirit and
in truth, for that is the kind of worship the Father wants." The
woman replies, "I know that the Messiah, that is the Christ, is
coming. When he comes he will tell us everything." Jesus said,
"I, who am talking to you, I am he."

What an extraordinary moment! It is the first time in this gospel that Jesus reveals his true identity to anyone. Something he
sees in her gives him the confidence to be so nakedly vulnerable;
and something she sees in him gives her the confidence to follow his lead, to go higher and higher and deeper and deeper in
herself, knowing far beyond what she could know from ordinary
knowingness, knowing fully in the immediacy of her heart. This
quality of awareness is not something that comes from outside
the moment. Rather, it grows up in the moment itself through
the quality and energy of the heart connection. It is a transfusion from within ("one deep calling to another," in the words

of Psalm 42). It is pristine and clear, and it is the basis of all true belief.

Bruno has some beautiful words to say about the nature of this transfusion a few paragraphs further along in *Second Simplicity*. He, too, has been reflecting on the mysterious energy of the exchange between Jesus and this unknown woman at the well, and he observes: "This Jesus whom we encounter is a light at the center of the world, a fire at the world's edge. He moves beneath the images of himself as an alternate center of energy. He awakens that which lies at the core of my own being. The series of Jesus's healings in the gospels are the story of the gradual raising to life and consciousness, to freedom and fullness, of this nascent person that I am."[5] He then concludes with this remarkable statement: "The knowledge of Jesus Christ is a unitive knowledge; it is the luminosity of my own true and eternal being."[6] In other words, to quote Psalm 36, "in your light we see light." Jesus Christ standing before the Samaritan woman becomes the mirror in which she sees not only the face of God but her own true face.

In the gospels, all the people who encountered Jesus only by hearsay, by what somebody else believed about him, by what they'd been told, by what they hoped to get out of him: all those people left. They still leave today. The ones that remained—and still remain—are the ones who have met him in the moment: in the instantaneous, mutual recognition of hearts and in the ultimate energy that is always pouring forth from this encounter. It is indeed the wellspring.

2

Jesus in Context

THERE'S A STORY, purportedly true, of a school board in the heart of the Tennessee Bible belt wrestling with whether or not to institute a foreign-language curriculum in its high school. After heated discussion, the debate was finally brought to an end when one board member stood up and said, "No way! If English was good enough for Jesus Christ, it's good enough for my son."

We can laugh, of course, but the laughter is a trifle nervous; for most of us, it's more a matter of degree than kind. The majority of Christians are still decidedly more comfortable reciting the Lord's Prayer or Twenty-third Psalm in the old King James Version than in the many new translations now available (my well-educated grandmother insisted that prayer sounded holier when spoken in "thees" and "thous"). And one Sunday morning when I offered the Lord's Prayer in the original Aramaic of Jesus, several members of my congregation were distinctly troubled. "It sounded *Islamic*," one woman worried.

Jesus was a Near Eastern event. We need to keep reminding ourselves of this. When the meteor of his being tumbled into time and space it landed in Palestine, not in Elizabethan England. From Palestine, of course, its influence radiated out in all directions. One line came west, carried by the apostle Paul through Turkey and into the Greco-Roman lands. That's the line we're most familiar with. But the energy also traveled in directions that we know a lot less about. Another line went southwest to Africa and from there jumped across the Strait of Gibraltar and traveled up the west coast of France to the Celtic strongholds of Brittany and Ireland. Still another line radiated east into Persia, India, and even China. And the energy certainly stayed right there in the Middle East, in lands that are today primarily Islamic: Iraq, Syria, and Turkey. All of these energy streams flowing out from the Jesus event had their unique flavors—and they are very different from the flavor we're used to in our own stream.

Back even fifty years ago the whole picture seemed a lot simpler. We had the Bible (and for most people this meant the King James Bible); we had tradition; we had our creeds; we had our rules; we had our story line right. What was conveyed through the above channels was orthodox; what was not was heresy. And yes, some Christians did see things from differing viewpoints: there were Catholics and Protestants, and when they tried to converse with each other, this was known as ecumenism. Even today, the great majority of North Americans still experience Christians as coming in only two flavors: Catholic or Protestant. Many of us will have heard of the Greek and Russian Orthodox churches— although that is pretty much the limit of the known Christian universe. But what about the Ethiopian church? The Oriental Orthodox? The Nestorians? The ancient Syriacs? The Malabar Christians? The Chinese Christians of Xian with their distinctly Buddhist-flavored versions of the teachings of Jesus?[1] What do we know of all these other Christian streams of influence?

It's easy to be dismissive, of course—to simply shake our heads and say, "That's all gnostic." "Gnostic" is a term we love to hate. We don't exactly know what it means, but the one thing we do know is that anything labeled "gnostic" is not scriptural and not orthodox; there's something suspect about it. Later in this chapter I will try to shed some light on the words "gnostic" and "gnosticism." For now, suffice it to say that when we use these terms so disparagingly, we're actually exposing our deeply entrenched habit of viewing the Christian world through an exclusively Western filter—and of course, what this really means is that we're looking at it through a *Roman* filter. The two chief earmarks of the Roman filter are that it tends to confuse unity with uniformity and it puts a high priority on order and authority. You can see how over the centuries these two tendencies have played out in the Western Church.

Speaking of orthodoxy, a lot of Christians assume that the word *orthodox* means right belief. It's all about catechisms and creeds: believing the right things about Jesus, believing the way the church teaches you to believe. And yes, the word does etymologically derive from the Greek *ortho* (right) and *dokeo* (to think)—or in other words, it means "right thinking." But intuitively, I prefer to derive the "dox" part from the word *doxa,* which means "glory" (as in "Glory be to the Father and to the Son and to the Holy Spirit," known as the doxology). Orthodox would then mean "right glory" (or "right praise"), and while this may be linguistically, well, *unorthodox,* it does come a lot closer to conveying the spiritual ambience of most of non-Roman Christianity (or in other words, the other 270 degrees of the Jesus-event arc). Particularly for the Near Eastern Christians, there was a strong sense that belief was not something that should be pinned down too tightly, like angels dancing on the head of a pin. People come from all different backgrounds and all different levels of spiritual maturity, and belief will fluctuate accordingly. But what should properly hold the body of Christ together is *right praise,* the ability to transcend all these differing viewpoints and in one voice (though maybe varied harmonies) offer glory and thanksgiving to the Master whose life transforms the human heart. Whatever the literal meaning of the term "orthodox," this is its authentic spiritual meaning.

In the West, as I said, we early on lost that generosity of spirit. Because of the rigid, control-oriented focus built into our Western filter, we struggle even to comprehend (yet alone accept) the vibrancy, breadth, diversity, and inclusiveness of early

Christianity. We'll need to regain some of that breadth of vision before it's possible even to entertain the notion of Jesus as a wisdom master, because some of ideas I will be presenting in support of it are slightly unorthodox if we stick with a Protestant, evangelical, Western definition of what orthodox means. But as we allow ourselves to open to the wealth of new information and insights now coming our way, we begin to realize how tight a box we've been living in.

In the Wake of Nag Hammadi

It is no exaggeration to say that since the mid-twentieth century our Western map of the known Christian universe has been blasted wide open. From at least four directions new evidence has been streaming in to suggest that we are long overdue for a fundamental reevaluation of our understanding of the Jesus event. While some conservative Christians still balk at the prospect, most of mainstream biblical scholarship has gotten on board. There is simply too much new information out there to ignore.

Heading the list of these new sources of information is a whole new set of primary scriptural materials discovered in the early to mid-twentieth century, primarily in Egypt. The most stunning of these is the Nag Hammadi Codex, a veritable treasure trove of early Christian sacred writings, many of them heretofore unknown, or known *of* but presumed to be lost forever. These priceless scrolls were found during the final days of World War II, carefully stored in a large urn in a cave near Nag Hammadi, along the upper Nile. In a great tale of international intrigue, they were smuggled out of Egypt, sequestered for a while in the manuscript collection of Carl Jung, and at last released to an international consortium of biblical scholars who could begin to edit and assess them. The work continues to this day, and it still occasionally makes media headlines.[2]

The first questions, of course, were, "What are these writings?

How did they get there?" The emerging scholarly consensus was that they had probably been placed there for safekeeping by an unknown monastic community late in the fourth century when the Christian theological climate underwent a sea change. These writings had once been part of the monastery's sacred scriptures—their "bible," so to speak, in those fluid early centuries before the contents of the New Testament were nailed down—but they had failed to make the cut among tightening standards of orthodoxy. In the year 367, Bishop Athanasius of Alexandria ordered the monks to destroy all writings not specifically designated as canonical. Heartsick at the thought, the monks sealed their treasure in a large clay time capsule until some wiser and kinder era when the contents could once again be appreciated.

The Nag Hammadi collection is a huge find, both in size and import. Among the many important early texts recovered here, probably the most significant is the Gospel of Thomas, which gives us a radically new take on Jesus and the metaphysics behind his teachings. (I will have much more to say on Thomas in chapter 5.) Scholars have been busy for several decades now evaluating these texts and assessing how they change our picture of early Christianity—which they do in big ways.

The second influence widening the picture for us has been a relatively new field of scholarly study known as Syriac studies, which came into its heyday in the 1960s and in its time was quite a high-tech enterprise. Scholars began to discover that if they scraped beneath the surface of certain later manuscripts (chiefly liturgical ceremonies) in use among Syrian-speaking Christians, they found a living record of oral traditions that had existed from the earliest Christian era—long before the church consolidated around its Byzantine base of orthodoxy. Since Jesus himself emerged out of this stream (Syrian as well as Jesus's native Aramaic are both part of the Semitic linguistic and cultural stream), these memories carried considerable weight. Surprisingly, the majority of these ancient recovered texts seemed to be closely associated with the ceremony of baptism, and when scholars began to look carefully at the underlying theology, they stared in disbelief. It was a drastically different take on who Jesus was and what his mission was all about.

The third major stream of influence also arrived from the desert at about the same time as the Nag Hammadi was found. It was the discovery, at Qumran, of the cache of writings commonly known as the Dead Sea Scrolls. Of course, these are not Christian texts. Scholars generally identify them as belonging to the Essene community, a mystical Jewish sect that encamped at Qumran and undertook rigorous ascetical practices in order to prepare for the Messiah's imminent return. The importance of these writings for our understanding of Jesus is that most scholars now feel that it was in this matrix of Jewish mystical expectation and millennialist fervor that Jesus's own sense of vocation was most immediately shaped. The discovery of these scrolls allows us to see Jesus more clearly within his own context. It also gives a distinctly different accent to his teachings as we realize how much of what he had to say was already deeply present in the apocalyptic yearning and ferment of the Judaism of his times.

Finally (and this may seem like it's out of left field, but in light of some of the things I was saying in the first chapter maybe you'll see that it's not), an important stream of insight once again available to us has come through the recovery of Christianity's own contemplative tradition. The past forty or so years have been an era of contemplative reawakening. Christian seekers now have at their disposal two authentically Christian methods of meditation: Centering Prayer and Christian Meditation. Centering prayer, the practice I myself have been trained in, was developed in the early 1970s by the Trappist monks of St. Joseph's Abbey in Spencer, Massachusetts, and has been further refined and popularized primarily by Father Thomas Keating. Tens of thousands of people worldwide now practice it daily. Meanwhile, there's at least that many practicing Christian Meditation, a parallel form of silent meditation developed in about the same era by the Benedictine abbot Dom John Main.

What does it mean to have tens of thousands of Christians

meditating? Quite a lot, because meditation is the universal and time-tested method for "putting the mind in the heart." It circumvents our preconceived expectations and mental agendas and opens up that place of immediate knowingness I spoke of in the last chapter, where we can directly experience the living Jesus. For the first four centuries of Christian experience, this is the way it was done; Christians connected with their living Master present in their hearts (the name for this practice was *anamnesis,* or "living remembrance"). That's the skill set, if you want to put it in those terms, which meditation once again makes available to us. The early church fathers used to speak of a pathway of perception they called *epinoia,* which meant knowing through intuition and direct revelation, not through the linear and didactic *dianoia* of logic and doctrine and dogma.[3] Sixteen centuries later we're learning the process all over again. And when we do so, we can begin to see through our own eyes what those early Christians saw. This inner seeing brings an important second line of bearing to all these wonderful new texts, resources, and treasure troves that the past five decades have bestowed upon us.

Savior or Life-Giver?

What emerges from this new picture? The main difference between the Christianity we're familiar with through our Western filter and the Christianity coming to us from these new sources can be captured in two words which are not nearly as formidable as they first sound: the difference is between a *soteriology* and a *sophiology.*

What do these two words mean? "Soteriology" comes from the Greek word *soter,* which means "savior." The Christianity of the West has always been savior-oriented. Jesus is seen as the one who died for our sins, who rescued us both individually and corporately from the exile and alienation brought about through the disobedience of Adam and Eve. "Do you believe Christ died for your sins?" is still the core question for Christian orthodoxy:

the dividing line between a believer and a nonbeliever. This emphasis entered the theology of the West early, and it entered through the apostle Paul.

You probably remember Paul's story. (If not, you'll find it in the first several chapters of the book of Acts.) Prior to his conversion, Paul (then known as Saul) was an adamant foe of Christianity. He was a Pharisee and a perfectionist, intent on observing every detail of the Jewish law. Privately he was clearly worried that something in his being was dark and damaged (he mentions this from time to time in his epistles), but seeing no other options, he was trying his best to work out his salvation through a meticulous observance of the Law. Such was his state when, en route to Damascus to persecute Christians, he had a powerful visionary encounter with the risen Jesus in which he experienced himself as forgiven and saved. That dramatic experience became the emotional epicenter of all his theological reflection, and as he traveled west on his missionary journeys, he carried it with him.

Four centuries later history repeated itself, with a person only slightly less influential to the course of Christianity in the West: Augustine of Hippo. Like Paul, he had been trying to save his soul by meticulously following a path—in his case, a path of gnostic esotericism. And he, too, found himself suddenly transported out of his complicated metaphysics and brooding self-hatred into the radiant presence of Christ. Augustine's personal experience of the contrast between human darkness and the light of Christ eventually found expression in his doctrine of original sin. Over time that contrast got even more accentuated, to the point where a strong vein of Western spirituality began to speak of "the total depravity of man." This mindset continues to have a powerful hold on the West today; it is still the underlying theology that many Christians grew up with. I continue to be dismayed at the number of times during a Centering Prayer workshop that I mention the divine indwelling ("The Kingdom of Heaven is within you"), only to have someone in the audience vigorously correct me: "No, human beings are totally sinful; nothing of God lives within us." It's all hopeless unless we believe in Jesus and put our full trust in his mercy— that's the slant in the Christianity of the West.

The Christianity of the East saw things radically differently. Theirs was not a soteriology, but a sophiology. The word "sophiology" has as its root the word "wisdom." (*Sophia* is the Greek word for wisdom.) Christianity was supremely a wisdom path. For the earliest Christians, Jesus was not the Savior but the Life-Giver. In the original Aramaic of Jesus and his followers there was no word for salvation. Salvation was understood as a bestowal of life, and to be saved was "to be made alive."[4] Entering the waters at the hand of John the Baptist, Jesus emerged as *Muhyana*, "the Life-Giver." He came forth also as the Ihidaya, "the Single One" or "the Unified One." Nowadays we'd call him "the Enlightened One," a person whose life is full, integrated, and flowing. Jesus's disciples saw in him a master of consciousness, offering a path through which they, too, could become *ihidaya*, enlightened ones. A sophiological Christianity focuses on the path. It emphasizes how Jesus is like us, how what he did in himself is something we are also called to do in ourselves. By contrast, soteriology tends to emphasize how Jesus is different from us—"begotten, not made," belonging to a higher order of being—and hence uniquely positioned as our mediator.

At first the sophiological take may seem strange to you: definitely a variant and perhaps even a heretical position. But as the evidence begins to pour in from the other 270 degrees of the Christian circle, we begin to see that it is the West that holds the variant position. From the Gospel of Thomas and the Nag Hammadi collection in general, from the Syriac liturgies, from the African desert fathers and mothers, from Celtic poetry and Chinese "Jesus sutras" the same sophiological message emerges. "Yes," says Jesus, "as I am, you, too, can and must become. I will be here to help you. But you must do the work yourself." Whatever theological premises you may or may not choose to believe about Jesus, the primary task of a Christian is not to believe theological premises but to put on the mind of Christ.[5]

The Gnostic Gnemesis

While we're on the subject of sophiology, let me say just a little bit more about the notoriously treacherous terms "gnostic" and "gnosticism." The word "gnostic" is simply the adjective form of the word "gnosis," which means "knowledge." *Sophia* and *gnosis* are more or less synonyms. They both imply an integral, participational knowledge carried not in one's head but in one's entire being. (In fact, the Hebrew equivalent for these terms is *da'ath*, which is the same word used for "lovemaking"—as in "David entered Bathsheba's tent and 'knew' her.") "Gnosis" is a perfectly acceptable New Testament word; the apostle Paul uses it repeatedly in his attempts to describe the intimate experience of knowing and being known in Christ.

In this broader sense, then, all sophiological Christianity is gnostic. And Jesus is definitely gnostic himself.

Where we get into trouble is when we confuse this broader meaning of the word "gnosis" with a late and specifically Greek heresy that began to affect Christianity during the second and third centuries and became the subject of considerable fulmination from the early church fathers. In this more restricted usage, Gnosticism is dualistic, top-heavy with nouns (like most Greek philosophy), and metaphysically complex, and it tends to confuse integral knowing with esoteric information, often conveyed through secret initiatic rituals. In this sense, sophiology is definitely *not* Gnostic.

To further complicate the subject, you'll sometimes find teachings where these two streams seem to overlap—as, for example, in the Gospel of Mary Magdalene, where some of the gnostic metaphysical language is used but within a clearly Semitic spiritual context. The confusion can be solved on a case-by-case basis once one realizes that Gnosticism (capital G) is the distortion that inevitably results when one tries to download gnosis (integral knowing) into exclusively mental constructs. To reject the entire rich and authentic tradition of Christian sophiology (as many Christian fundamentalists are wont to do) on the basis of the scare word "gnosticism" is like throwing out the baby with the bathwater.

Wisdom and Wisdom Teachers

When I talk about Jesus as a wisdom master, I need to mention yet another feature of the Near Eastern context unlike our own. In the Near East, "wisdom teacher" is a recognized spiritual occupation. That's not so in the West. I remember how back in seminary I was taught that there were only two categories of religious authority within the Judaic tradition: one could be a priest or a prophet. That indeed may be the way the tradition has filtered down to us in the West. But within the spiritual traditions of the wider Near East (including Judaism itself), there was also a third, albeit unofficial category: what I call the *moshel moshelim*, or teacher of wisdom, the one who taught the ancient traditions of the transformation of the human being. These teachers of transformation, among whom I would place the authors of the Hebrew wisdom literature such as Ecclesiastes, Job, and Proverbs, may be the early precursors to the *rabbi* whose task it was to interpret the law and lore of Judaism (often creating their own innovations of each.) The hallmark of these wisdom teachers was their use of pithy sayings, puzzles, and parables rather than prophetic pronouncements or divine decree. They spoke to people in the language that people spoke, the language of story rather than law.

How do we know that Jesus was seen as a wisdom teacher? Aside from the fact that throughout the gospels people spontaneously address him as "Rabbi," I can make my point by asking this simple question: "What literary form do you associate with Jesus's teachings?" Most people will immediately say, "Parables." Correct—and parables are a wisdom genre. They belong to *mashal*, the Jewish branch of the universal tradition of sacred poetry, stories, proverbs, riddles, and dialogues through which wisdom is conveyed. A person who teaches in parables is teaching within a wisdom tradition. As we shall see shortly, Jesus not only taught within the tradition, he turned it end for end. But before we can appreciate the extraordinary nuances he brought to his understanding of human transformation, we need first to know something about the stream he was working in.

There has always been a strong tendency among Christians to turn him into a priest—"our great high priest," in the powerful metaphor of the New Testament Letter to the Hebrews. The image of Christos Pantokrator ("Lord of All Creation") dressed in splendid sacramental robes has dominated the iconography of both Eastern and Western Christendom. But Jesus was not a priest. He had nothing to do with the temple hierarchy in Jerusalem, and he kept a respectful distance from most ritual observances. Nor was he a prophet in the usual sense of the term: a messenger sent to the people of Israel to warn them of impending political catastrophe in an attempt to redirect their hearts to God. Jesus was not interested in the political fate of Israel, nor would he accept the role of Messiah continuously being thrust upon him. His message was not one of repentance and return to the covenant. Rather, he stayed close to the perennial ground of wisdom: the transformation of human consciousness. He asked those timeless and deeply personal questions: What does it mean to die before you die? How do you go about losing your little life to find the bigger one? Is it possible to live on this planet with a generosity, abundance, fearlessness, and beauty that mirror Divine Being itself? These are the wisdom questions, and they are the entire field of Jesus's concern. If you look for a comparable category today, the closest analogy would probably be the Sufi *sheik,* who wields the threefold functions of wisdom teacher, spiritual elder, and channel for the direct transmission of blessing (*baraka*), in a fashion closely parallel to Jesus's himself. The sheik is a distinctly Near Eastern category, and it probably best preserves the mantle that Jesus himself once wore.

Jesus Was Not a Hick

As we conclude this revisioning exercise, one other thing needs to be said in order to adjust the filters through which we look at Jesus. Within our Western tradition there has been a strong tendency to sentimentalize Jesus as an uneducated tradesman. After all, didn't he grow up in a small town in Galilee as a humble carpenter's son? We're actually somewhat invested in this fantasy, because it strengthens our case that he learned what he learned directly from God. But when you read the Bible carefully, the picture doesn't hold up.

First of all, we need to recognize the implications of the fact that Jesus grew up in Galilee, not in Jerusalem. We tend to think of Jerusalem as the cultural center and that going up to Jerusalem from the Galilean lands was like going from Appalachia to New York City. But in point of fact, it was the other way around. Far from being a cultural backwater, Galilee was actually the more cosmopolitan environment because it lay on the Silk Road, that great viaduct of human commerce which from time immemorial has connected the lands of the Mediterranean with the lands and culture of Central Asia and China. The Silk Road went right through the city of Capernaum, where Jesus did a lot of his learning and his teaching. It was an environment in which he would have been fully exposed to a variety of ideas that could be seen as the New Age of his time. And Jesus evidently soaked up spiritual teaching like a sponge. While he was definitely his own person, he was not operating in a cultural vacuum. His teachings show clear areas of overlap with the great stream of *sophia perennis* flowing through other spiritual traditions, particularly Buddhism and Persian light mysticism.[6]

Second, we know that he could read. We learn this right from the scriptures themselves, when we see him in Luke 4:16 walking into the synagogue in that great moment of his public debut, reading from the scrolls of the prophet Isaiah and then announcing, "Today this scripture has been fulfilled." He probably spoke several languages. We know for certain that he spoke Aramaic

and Hebrew, and we can pretty well infer that he understood
Latin (in light of his exchange with Pontius Pilate) and most
likely Greek. He was a literate citizen of his day.

Further, we know that he almost certainly had some sort of
religious training or apprenticeship. There has been a continuous effort to link him with the Essene community I spoke of
earlier, whose teachings and spiritual practices are recorded in
the Qumran scrolls. The Essenes were a Jewish ascetical sect,
rigorous in their pursuit of repentance and purification. There's
a very good chance that John the Baptist belonged to this sect.
And there's also a very good chance that Jesus came through
this training. He didn't finally stay with it, but it is highly likely
that he would have been exposed to it and known about it.

Of course, this diverse cultural background was merely the
springboard for his own original genius. He was not only a
teacher of wisdom, he was a master of wisdom. He is particularly
fond of taking a familiar saying or proverb and either pushing
it to the limit or overturning it altogether. We had a glimpse
already of how his mind works in the quotation from the Gospel
of Thomas at the beginning of the last chapter. In place of the
familiar "Seek and you shall find," he presents a complex sixfold
schematic of the spiritual search, encompassing both confusion
and wonder as necessary steps in the journey of reintegration.
And in one of his most familiar but challenging teachings in
Luke, he takes even the Golden Rule to its outer limits, pushing
beyond all traces of enlightened self-interest into a no-holds-
barred exhortation to love without counting the cost:

> But I say to you that listen, Love your enemies, do good
> to those who hate you . . . Do to others as you would
> have them do to you. If you love those who love you,
> what credit is that to you? For even sinners love those
> who love them. If you do good to those who do good
> to you, what credit is that to you? For even sinners do
> the same. If you lend to those from whom you hope
> to receive, what credit is that to you? Even sinners lend

to sinners, to receive as much again. But love your enemies, do good, and lend, expecting nothing in return . . . Be merciful, just as your Father is merciful. (Luke 6:27–28, 31–36)

We can see the razor edge of his brilliance as he takes the familiar world of *mashal* far beyond the safety zone of conventional morality into a world of radical reversal and paradox. He is transforming proverbs into parables—and a parable, incidentally, is not the same thing as an aphorism or a moral lesson. Its closest cousin is really the Buddhist koan, a deliberately subversive paradox aimed at turning our usual mind upside down. My colleague Lynn Bauman refers to parables as "spiritual hand grenades"; their job is not to confirm but to uproot. You can imagine the effect that had on his audience! Throughout the gospels we hear people saying again and again, "What is this he's teaching? No one has ever said anything like this before. Where did he get this? Where did he come from?"

Jesus's response to those questions was always the same: "Come and see." And this will be true for us as well as we prepare to follow him on his steeplechase. But in order to be able to keep him in sight, it is helpful to know where he is coming from. Within his authentic Near Eastern context he emerges as a sophisticated, fully attuned, and even cosmopolitan teacher, working in a genre that is recognized by his audience but teaching it so much more powerfully and boldly that he pulls people right up with a start. As we actually taste the flavor of what he's teaching, we begin to see that it's not proverbs for daily living, or ways of being virtuous. He's proposing a total meltdown and recasting of human consciousness, bursting through the tiny acorn-selfhood that we arrived on the planet with into the oak tree of our fully realized personhood. He pushes us toward it, teases us, taunts us, encourages us, and ultimately walks us there. How he does this will be the subject of our next chapter.

3

"The Kingdom of Heaven Is within You"

WHAT DID JESUS actually teach? Here is another place where the overfamiliarity that's bred into us as a Christian culture gets in our way. A well-known Southern Baptist theologian quips that the whole of his Sunday school training could be summed up in one sentence (delivered with a broad Texas drawl): "Jesus is *nice,* and he wants us to be nice, too."

Many of us have grown up with Jesus all our lives. We know a few of the parables, like those about the good Samaritan or the prodigal son. Some people can even quote a few of the beatitudes. Most everyone can stumble through the Lord's Prayer. But how often do you hear the teaching assessed a whole? When it comes to spiritual teachers from other traditions, it seems right and fair to ask what kind of path they're on. What does the Dalai Lama teach? What did Krishnamurti teach? How about Adyashanti? But we never ask this question about Jesus. Why not? When we actually get below the surface of his teaching, we find there's a lot more going on than meets the eye. A whole lot more. And it doesn't have much to do with being "nice."

One of the most important books to appear in recent years is called *Putting on the Mind of Christ*, by a man named Jim Marion, who, remarkably, is not a theologian but a Washington lawyer.[1] His title is a statement in itself. "Putting on the mind of Christ" is a direct reference to St. Paul's powerful injunction in Philippians 2:5: "Let the same mind be in you that was in Christ Jesus." The words call us up short as to what we are actually supposed to be doing on this path: not just admiring Jesus, but acquiring his consciousness.

It's true that for the better part of the past sixteen hundred years Christianity has put a lot more emphasis on the things we know *about* Jesus. In the last chapter I spoke about how the word "orthodox" has come to be interpreted as having the correct beliefs. Along with the overt requirement here (to learn what these beliefs are and agree with them) comes also a subliminal message: that the appropriate way to relate to Jesus is through a series of beliefs. In fundamentalist Christianity this message tends to get even more accentuated, to the point where faith essentially appears to be a matter of signing on the dotted lines to a series of creedal statements. Belief *in* Jesus is indistinguishable from belief *about* him.

But this certainly wasn't how it was done in the early church— nor can it ever be done this way if what we are really seeking is to come into a living relationship with this wisdom master. Jim Marion's book returns us to the right ballpark—to the central challenge Christianity ought to be handing us. Indeed, how do we put on the mind of Christ? How do we see through his eyes? How do we feel through his heart? How do we learn to respond to the world with that same wholeness and healing love? That's what Christian orthodoxy really is all about. It's not about right belief; it's about right practice.

Marion approaches this question from a very intriguing perspective. He notices that throughout his teachings, Jesus uses one particular phrase repeatedly: "the Kingdom of Heaven." You can easily confirm this yourself by a quick browse through the gospels; the words jump out at you from everywhere. "The Kingdom of Heaven is like this," "The Kingdom of Heaven is like that," "The Kingdom of Heaven is within you," "The Kingdom of Heaven is at hand." Whatever this Kingdom of Heaven is, it's of foundational importance to what Jesus is trying to teach.

So what do we take it to be? Biblical scholars have debated this question for almost as long as there have been biblical scholars. A lot of Christians, particularly of a more evangelical persuasion, assume that the Kingdom of Heaven means the place where you go when you die—if you've been good. But the problem with this interpretation is that Jesus himself specifically contradicts it when he says, "The Kingdom of Heaven is *within you*" (that is, here) and "*at hand*" (that is, now). It's not later, but *lighter*—some more subtle quality or dimension of experience accessible to you right in the moment. You don't die into it; you awaken into it.

The other approach people have consistently tried is to equate the Kingdom of Heaven with an earthly utopia. The Kingdom of Heaven would be a realm of peace and justice, where human beings lived together in harmony and fair distribution of economic assets. For thousands of years prophets and visionaries have labored to bring into being their respective versions of this second kind of Kingdom of Heaven, but somehow these earthly utopias never seem to stay put for very long. And here again, Jesus specifically rejected this meaning. When his followers wanted to proclaim him the Messiah, the divinely anointed king of Israel who would inaugurate the reign of God's justice upon the earth, Jesus shrank from all that and said, strongly and unequivocally, "My kingdom is not of this world."

Where is it, then? Jim Marion's wonderfully insightful and contemporary suggestion is that the Kingdom of Heaven is really a metaphor for a *state of consciousness*; it is not a place you go to, but a place you *come from*. It is a whole new way of looking at the world, a transformed awareness that literally turns this world into a different place. Marion suggests specifically that the Kingdom of Heaven is Jesus's own favorite way of describing a state we would nowadays call a "nondual consciousness" or "unitive consciousness." The hallmark of this awareness is that it sees no separation—not between God and humans, not between humans and other humans. And these are indeed Jesus's two core teachings, underlying everything he says and does.

No separation between God and humans. When Jesus talks about this Oneness, he is not speaking in an Eastern sense about an equivalency of being, such that I am in and of myself divine.[2] What he more has in mind is a complete, mutual indwelling: I am in God, God is in you, you are in God, we are in each other. His most beautiful symbol for this is in the teaching in John 15 where he says, "I am the vine; you are the branches. Abide in me as I in you." A few verses later he says, "As the Father has loved me, so I have loved you. Abide in my love." While he does indeed claim that "the Father and I are one" (John 10:30)—a statement so blasphemous to Jewish ears that it nearly gets him stoned—he does not see this as an exclusive privilege but as something shared by all human beings. There is no separation between humans and God because of this mutual interabiding which expresses the indivisible reality of divine love. We flow into God—and God into us—because it is the nature of love to flow. And as we give ourselves into one another in this fashion, the vine gives life and coherence to the branch while the branch makes visible what the vine is. (After all, a vine is merely an abstraction until there are actual branches to articulate its reality.) The whole and the part live together in mutual, loving reciprocity, each belonging to the other and dependent on the other to show forth the fullness of love. That's Jesus's vision of no separation between human and Divine.

No separation between human and human is an equally powerful notion—and equally challenging. One of the most familiar of Jesus's teachings is "Love your neighbor as yourself." But we almost always hear that wrong. We hear "Love your neighbor *as much as* yourself." (And of course, the next logical question then becomes, "But I have to love me first, don't I, before I can love my neighbor?") If you listen closely to Jesus's teaching however, there is no "as much as" in there. It's just "Love your neighbor *as* yourself"—as a continuation of your very own being. It's a complete seeing that your neighbor is you. There are not two individuals out there, one seeking to better herself at the price of the other, or to extend charity to the other; there are simply two cells of the one great Life. Each of them is equally precious and necessary. And as these two cells flow into one another, experiencing that one Life from the inside, they discover that "laying down one's life for another" is not a loss of one's self but a vast expansion of it—because the indivisible reality of love is the only True Self.

These are the core points of a very radical teaching—not only light years ahead of its time but way ahead of our own as well. To demonstrate just *how* far ahead, Jim Marion makes helpful use of a schematic pioneered by one of the great philosophers of our own era, Ken Wilber. Wilber teaches that human consciousness exists along a nine-level continuum,[3] from the archaic consciousness of infants and early Stone Age peoples through the highest stages of nondual consciousness, the full enlightenment of the Ihidaya (or Single One) that we spoke about in the last chapter. In Jesus's times, most people were at about Stage Three, or "mythic" consciousness, their sense of identity oriented collectively around membership in a specific tribal group. Today a greater number of individuals have attained to Stage Four, or "rational" consciousness, and a few even to Stage Five, or "vision logic"—although when pushed by fear or uncertainty, the more primitive group mentality will still quickly reassert itself. So you can see the challenge, both then and now. In Jim Marion's take, Jesus comes as a master of nondual consciousness—probably the first that Western civilization had ever seen—calling people to a radical transformation of consciousness at least six stages above their heads, and still four or five above our own. No wonder it is difficult to catch the subtlety of his teaching!

But the fact that he did this—and continues to do so as we learn to open to his ongoing presence—suggests that this transformation is both possible and intended for human beings. And there may well be something in the teaching itself that allows these stages to unfold quickly, in a geometric rather than linear progression. As Jesus would say, "Come and see." But in any case, the Kingdom of Heaven is his pet metaphor for life lived out of this transformed consciousness. It's the world you bring into being when you see with the eye of singleness. And it actually exists. It's not just a metaphor, but a transfiguration of *this* realm through the power of Oneness.

The Egoic Operating System

I would like to reflect a bit more on this very rich idea of Jesus as a master of consciousness, approaching it this time from a slightly different angle with the help of a contemporary metaphor. One of the things I most appreciate about the computer era is that it furnishes us with a whole set of new and wonderful images with which to envision the spiritual life. So here's a computer metaphor: we human beings come into existence with a certain operating system already installed in us. We can make the choice to upgrade.

The system already installed in us is a binary operating system. It runs on the power of "either/or." People frequently call it the ego, but I prefer to stick with my metaphor and call it the "egoic operating system." It comes by its dualism honestly; the "binary operator," as it's called, is built right into the structure of the human brain.[4] The egoic operating system is really a grammar of perception, a way of making sense of the world by dividing the field into subject and object, inside and outside— and one of the most important first tasks of early childhood is to learn how to run the operating system. By the time she was one and a half, my granddaughter could already sing along with the Sesame Street jingle, "One of these things is not like the other," and pick out the cat from among three dogs. She didn't realize, of course, that this is really elementary training for her egoic operating system, which perceives through differentiation. How is a dog not like a cat? What makes a table different from a chair? What specific qualities make some particular thing unique? That's how the system works.

When we become aware of our identity using this egoic operating system, we experience ourselves as persons with distinct

qualities and attributes. When we introduce ourselves, we usually begin by listing these characteristics: "I am a Pisces, a six on
the enneagram, a person who loves the ocean, an Episcopalian,
a priest." We identify ourselves by putting on our identifiers,
that list of what makes us unique and special. And of course,
that same list also makes other people separate from me; they
are outside, and I'm inside. In this operating system I experience
myself as a distinct and fixed point of identity that "has" particular qualities and life experiences, and these things go to make
me who I am. That's what life looks like when seen through the
lens of the egoic operating system. It thinks in terms of good
and bad, right and wrong, before and after, up and down. And it
gives us a solid sense of ourselves as the one at the hub of all this
duality, the one inside mastering the experience.

A striking visual image of what this operating system is all
about presented itself to me recently when the last leg of my
flight from Seattle home to Aspen, Colorado, was aboard a
small commuter prop jet. We boarded just after sunset, and as
we prepared to push back from the gate, the pilot revved the
engine and a landing light came on. When the light hit the arc
of the quickly revolving propeller blade, suddenly a golden circle
appeared right outside my cabin window—an orb or disc that
had depth, dimension, density, solidity. I had to keep reminding
myself that it really didn't. It was just a mirage created by a very
fast-moving blade being backlit by a light.

Our sense of identity generated through the egoic operating system is exactly the same, and the great religious traditions
have said this all along. It's a mirage, an illusion. There is no
such self. There is no small self, no egoic being, no thing that's
separated from everything else, that has insides and outsides,
that has experiences. All these impressions are simply a function
of an operating system that has to divide the world up into bits
and pieces in order to perceive it. Like the great wisdom teachers
of all spiritual traditions, Jesus calls us beyond the illusion: "Hey,
you can upgrade your operating system, and life is going to look
a whole lot different when you do it."

Later I will return to the question of why we humans seem

to come with this binary operating system installed in the first place. I think it does have some real importance in the cosmic role we are asked to play; it's not a mistake. But for now let's just say that most people get stuck in it. That's who we think we are. We walk through our lives perceiving, reacting to, and attempting to negotiate the world "out there" on the basis of this operating system. It's like being lost in a mirage. A system based in duality can't possibly perceive oneness; it can't create anything beyond itself—only more duality and more trouble. So the drama goes on and on.

But we do have the capacity, if we so choose, to shift to a whole different basis of perception. We come into this life with another operating system already lying in latency, and if we wish to move in this direction, we can learn to steer by it, understand through it, and ultimately discover our deepest sense of identity within it.

Seeing with the Eye of the Heart

This other operating system (we can call it the nondual system or the unitive system, if we want) is the operating system of the heart. The egoic operating system is particularly related to the mind, to the "binary operator" built right into the human brain. The heart has a different way of perceiving. Rather than dividing and conquering, it connects with a seamless and indivisible reality through a whole different way of organizing the informational field. And it's ours for the choosing.

Let's talk a bit about this other system. I used the word "heart" to describe it, and that probably requires some deconditioning, because in the West we customarily see the heart in a very clichéd and sentimental way. We play it off against the mind, so that a person is "in his head" if he's wedded to cerebral thinking and "in his heart" if he is oriented toward feeling. We almost always think of the heart as the center of our personal emotional life. But this is not the way the wisdom tradition sees it. In wisdom, the heart is primarily *an organ of spiritual perception*, a

highly sensitive instrument for keeping us aligned, as we journey
along the horizontal axis of our life in time, with the vertical axis
of timeless reality: the realm of meaning, value, and conscience.
The heart picks up reality in a much deeper and more integral
way than our poor, Cartesian minds even begin to imagine. The
contemporary Sufi teacher Kabir Helminski offers the following
definition, which encapsulates in a wonderfully precise way what
universal wisdom has always known about the heart:

> We have subtle subconscious faculties we are not using.
> Beyond the limited analytic intellect is a vast realm of
> mind that includes psychic and extrasensory abilities;
> intuition; wisdom; a sense of unity; aesthetic, qualita-
> tive and creative faculties; and image-forming and sym-
> bolic capacities. Though these faculties are many, we
> give them a single name with some justification, because
> they are operating best when they are in concert. They
> comprise a mind, moreover, in spontaneous connection
> with the cosmic mind, the total mind we call "heart."[5]

The heart can pick up subtle signals from all levels of reality,
not just from what's happening in the rational. The intellect is a
part of it, you notice; but the field of perception goes far beyond
just the rational. The heart picks up from the emotions, from
our sense of proportion, from intuition, from images and archetypes. And most important—as we saw in chapter 1—it keeps us
aligned with our innermost, with what we truly know.

Unlike the egoic operating system, the heart does not perceive through differentiation. It doesn't divide the field into
inside and out, subject and object. Rather, it perceives by means
of harmony. It's like hearing the note G played and instantly
hearing a D and a B around it that make it into a chord, that
join it to a whole. When heart-awareness becomes fully formed
within a person, he or she will be operating out of nondual consciousness. But it's not simply a higher level of the same old
mind; it's a whole new operating system! That person does
indeed see from a perspective of singleness—and just as Jesus

called for, there is now no separation between God and humans, or between humans and other humans, simply because separation isn't factored into the new operating system. It is no longer necessary for perception, so it simply falls away like scales from the eyes.

This seems like a very fruitful approach to the teachings of Jesus. "Blessed are the pure [that is, single] of heart, for they shall see God," he says in the beatitudes, but who would have believed that he is not talking about perfecting one's virtue but about upgrading the operating system! And yet the metaphor seems to work and brings an underlying coherence to what he is about. His whole mission can fundamentally be seen as trying to push, tease, shock, and wheedle people beyond the "limited analytic intellect" of their egoic operating system into the "vast realm of mind" where they will discover the resources they need to live in fearlessness, coherence, and compassion—or in other words, as true human beings.

There's an interesting confirmation of this from an unexpected quarter. You'll often hear, in connection with the teachings of Jesus, that he came to this earth calling us to repentance. "Repent" is a very popular word in our Christian lexicon, particularly in evangelical and fundamentalist quarters—"Repent, for the day of the Lord is at hand." But what does the word actually mean? The answer may surprise you.

The Greek that it's translating is *metanoia*. And guess what? It doesn't mean feeling sorry for yourself for doing bad things. It doesn't even mean to "change the direction in which you're looking for happiness," although it's often translated that way.[6] The word literally breaks down into *meta* and *noia*, which, depending on how you translate *meta* (it can be either the preposition "beyond" or the adjective "large"), means "go beyond the mind" or "go into the large mind."[7] The repentance that Jesus really is talking about means to go beyond your little egoic operating system that says, "I think, therefore I am," and try out the other one—the big one—that says, "I am, therefore I think."

I sometimes joke with my Centering Prayer students that when they sit down to do their twenty minutes of meditation, they are really engaged in an exercise in repentance. It's true, if you take *metanoia* in this alternative sense. They are going beyond their minds, into the larger mind. And Jesus, the master of repentance, is leading them there.

Christians aren't commonly used to hearing that Jesus was really about transforming our operating system. Admittedly, it's an unusual take on the subject. But one of his parables speaks to this clash of operating systems in a way that is simply unmistakable: the notoriously challenging laborers in the vineyard (Matthew 20:1–15). Nearly every Christian I've ever met has found that this parable is by far the most difficult of Jesus's teachings to understand and accept. You'll see why when you read it:

> The kingdom of heaven is like a landowner who went out early in the morning to hire laborers for his vineyard. After agreeing with the laborers for the usual daily wage, he sent them into his vineyard. When he went out about nine o'clock, he saw others standing idle in the marketplace; and he said to them, 'You also go into the vineyard, and I will pay you whatever is right." So they went. When he went out again about noon and about three o'clock, he did the same. And about five o'clock he went out and found others standing around; and he said to them, "Why are you standing here idle all day?" They said to him, "Because no one has hired us." He said to them, "You also go into the vineyard." When evening came, the owner of the vineyard said to his manager, "Call the laborers and give them their pay, beginning with the last and then going to the first." When those hired about five o'clock came, each of them received the usual daily wage. Now when the first came, they thought they would receive more; but each of them also received the usual daily wage. And when they received it, they grumbled against the landowner, saying, "These last worked only one hour, and you have made them equal to us who have borne the burden of the day and the scorching heat." But he replied to one

of them, "Friend, I am doing you no wrong; did you not agree with me for the usual daily wage? Take what belongs to you and go; I choose to give to this last the same as I give to you. Am I not allowed to do what I choose with what belongs to me? Or are you envious because I am generous?"

Probably more than any other teaching in the gospels, this parable tends to defy all logic and common sense. People unanimously exclaim, "It's not fair!" I once, in fact, heard a sermon on this parable by a preacher who began, "That's all well and good in the gospel, but in *real* life human beings deserve a fair wage." But from the point of view of consciousness training, it begins to make sense. This is perhaps Jesus's most koan-like parable: As long as you're using the egoic operating system, you just can't get it. You will see the owner's action as unfair because you're keeping track of more or less, better or worse, first versus last. And that is a function of the operating system you're using. The binary mind always perceives from a sense of scarcity and keeps track of the score through comparison and contrast. If the situation looks unfair to you, this is an infallible litmus test that you are still in your binary mind.

The only way you can "crack" this parable is to shift your perspective so that you see the glass as half full rather than half empty. When you approach the story from the perspective of fullness, you see that there's enough for everybody, that the good of everyone has been tended, and that all along it had never been a question of competition, but an invitation to participation and exchange. But that kind of seeing is only accessible within that other operating system, the nondual knowingness of the heart. This parable does indeed offer fair warning that what Jesus is up to is hugely more subversive than "Jesus is nice and he wants us to be nice too." Like any good Zen master, he is out to completely short-circuit our mental wiring so that we are catapulted into a whole new way of seeing and being.

If this is unsettling in itself, the corollary is even more disturbing: that until this mind shift has taken place, it's virtually impossible to live the teaching he has given us. In fact, I would say that it's flat-out impossible. One of the areas in which Christians have sadly deluded themselves, I believe, is in the sense that they have a franchise on the gospel, that they know how to do it. This is a very, very high teaching. Probably Jesus was the first in the Near Eastern lands to model this nondual or unitive teaching. We've been undercutting it ever since. The catch-22 for most Christians is that we're trying to do a nondual teaching with a dual mind. Until we are able to shift our operating system (both individually and collectively), we're always going to find ourselves in a position of hypocrisy and burnout.

I once knew an Anglican priest who was at the forefront of the civil rights movement in Philadelphia, a tireless champion of racial equality. Yet he slept with a baseball bat next to his bed in his west Philadelphia house so that none of *them* would get in and steal his goods. We all live with this terrible, heart-breaking hypocrisy in Christianity, when the teaching finally leaves us in the dust. How do we die before we die? How do we love our neighbors as ourselves? How do we bridge the gap between what we believe and what we can actually live? I believe that Jesus does leave us with a path for getting across that gap. We will be exploring it very shortly; it's what this book is principally all about. But honesty begins with admitting the gap exists. The attempt to make the gap invisible, as in so much of Christianity—thinking that because we believe it or can preach about it or know where in the gospels it's written, therefore we can do it—only leads us further into denial. This path has been attained by only a very enlightened few, the St. Francises of the world, the Mother Teresas of the world. And when it's attained, it's always in the same way: by somehow managing to fall all the way through the egoic operating system, with its inherent rigidity and fear, into the fullness of love that can be known only in and through the heart. How we do this will begin to unfold in the next chapter.

4

The Path of *Metanoia*

R EPENT, FOR THE END of the world is at hand! We use
the term "repent" extensively in our Christian vocabulary, usually meaning by it to confess our sins, acknowledge how
far off course we've wandered, and promise to turn our lives in
a new direction. But as I said in the previous chapter, the word
metanoia, usually translated as "repentance," literally means to
go "beyond the mind" or "into the larger mind." It means to
escape from the orbit of the egoic operating system, which by
virtue of its own internal hardwiring is always going to see the
world in terms of polarized opposites, and move instead into
that nondual knowingness of the heart which can see and live
from the perspective of wholeness. This is the central message of
Jesus. This is what his Kingdom of Heaven is all about. "Let's
get into the larger mind," he says. "This is what it looks like.
This is how you do it. Here, I'll help you . . ."

I realize that this interpretation of Jesus's teaching is probably
not what you grew up with in Sunday school. So what I'd like to
do now is to review some of those familiar teachings of Jesus—
the ones you learned as a child—and see if you hear a different

sort of ring to them when we approach them not as little moral lessons but as radical calls to the transformation of your consciousness. We'll begin with the most well known of these teachings, then move into turf that is perhaps much less familiar.

The Beatitudes (Matthew 5:1–12)

If you were raised Christian, you are probably familiar with the beatitudes. They're one of the "top three" texts that you get to memorize in Sunday school (along with the Ten Commandments and the Twenty-third Psalm). These eight short sayings (called "beatitudes" because they all begin with the phrase "Blessed are . . .") lay out Jesus's core teachings in a wonderfully concentrated and compelling format. Curiously, of all his teachings they are also the *least* commentated upon by the church fathers and theologians[1]—most likely, as we shall soon see, because they are clearly nondual teachings of the highest order, and most of the church still isn't there yet. Let's consider each of them in turn.

"Blessed are the poor in spirit, for theirs is the kingdom of heaven." From a wisdom perspective (that is, from the point of view of the transformation of consciousness), "poor in spirit" designates an inner attitude of receptivity and openness, and one is blessed by it because only in this state is it possible to receive anything. There's a wonderful Zen story that exactly translates this teaching. A young seeker, keen to become the student of a certain master, is invited to an interview at the master's house. The student rambles on about all his spiritual experience, his past teachers, his insights and skills, and his pet philosophies. The master listens silently and begins to pour a cup of tea. He pours and pours, and when the cup is overflowing he keeps right on pouring. Eventually the student notices what's going on and interrupts his monologue to say, "Stop pouring! The cup is full." The teacher says, "Yes, and so are you. How can I possibly teach you?"

This first beatitude speaks to that principle. In one of his most

beautiful insights, the contemporary Christian mystic Thomas
Merton once wrote, "At the center point of our being is a point
of nothingness which is untouched by sin and illusion, a point
of pure truth, a point of spark which belongs entirely to God."[2]
From time immemorial wisdom teaching has insisted that only
through that point of nothingness can we enter the larger mind.
As long as we're filled with ourselves, we can go no further.

   "Blessed are those who mourn, for they will be comforted." Essentially, from a wisdom perspective, this second beatitude is
talking about vulnerability and flow. When we mourn (and we're
talking about true mourning here, not complaining or self-
pity) we are in a state of freefall, our heart reaching out toward
what we have seemingly lost but cannot help loving anyway. To
mourn is by definition to live between the realms. "Practice the
wound of love," writes Ken Wilber in *Grace and Grit*, his grip-
ping personal story of loss and transformation. "Real love hurts;
real love makes you totally vulnerable and open; real love will
take you far beyond yourself; and therefore real love will dev-
astate you."[3] Mourning is indeed a brutal form of emptiness.
But in this emptiness, if we can remain open, we discover that a
mysterious "something" does indeed reach back to comfort us;
the tendrils of our grief trailing out into the unknown become
intertwined in a greater love that holds all things together. To
mourn is to touch directly the substance of divine compassion.
And just as ice must melt before it can begin to flow, we, too,
must become liquid before we can flow into the larger mind.
Tears have been a classic spiritual way of doing this.

   "Blessed are the meek, for they will inherit the earth" is how
the third beatitude is usually translated. A better translation
is "Blessed are the gentle," and perhaps an even better one is
"Blessed are the gentled." Remember that wonderful passage
from *The Little Prince* when the fox asks, "To tame something:
what does that mean?" The prince replies, " It means to form
bonds. If I tame you, I become responsible for you, and you
depend on me because I have tamed you."[4] That's the ballpark this beatitude is working in. Blessed are the ones who have
become spiritually "domesticated": the ones who have tamed

the wild animal energy within them, the passions and compulsions of our lower nature. In the Gospel of Thomas we will hear this process described as "devouring the lion"—because otherwise the lion will devour us! Only when we have dealt directly with our animal instincts, and the pervasive sense of fear and scarcity that emerge out of our egoic operating system, are we truly able to inherit the earth rather than destroying it.

"Blessed are those who hunger and thirst for righteousness, for they will be filled." The key to this fourth beatitude lies in understanding what the word "righteousness" means. To our post-Puritan, post-Victorian ears, righteousness is a synonym for virtue. It means being moral, behaving correctly. But in Israel of Jesus's times, righteousness was something much more dynamic than that. You can actually visualize it as a force field: an energy-charged sphere of holy presence. To be "in the righteousness of God" (as Old Testament writers are fond of saying) means to be directly connected to this vibrational field, to be anchored within God's own aliveness. There is nothing subtle about the experience; it is as fierce and intransigent a bond as picking up a downed electrical wire. To "hunger and thirst after righteousness," then, speaks to this intensity of connectedness. Jesus promises that when the hunger arises within you to find your own deepest aliveness within God's aliveness, it will be satisfied—in fact, the hunger itself is a sign that the bond is already in place. As we enter the path of transformation, the most valuable thing we have working in our favor is our yearning. Some spiritual teachers will even say that the yearning you feel for God is actually coming from the opposite direction; it is in fact God's yearning for *you.* "The eye with which you see God is the eye with which God sees you," said Meister Eckhart, one of the greatest Christian mystics, stressing the complete simultaneity of the energy of connection. When we yearn, we come into sympathetic vibration with a deeper heart-knowing. I spoke in the previous chapter about how the heart is an organ of alignment; it connects us. Yearning is the vibration of that connectedness. In this beatitude Jesus is not talking about doing virtuous deeds

so you'll be rewarded later; he is talking about being in connection with your fundamental yearning.

"Blessed are the merciful, for they will receive mercy." In this beatitude Jesus again returns to the idea of flow. Notice that there's an exchange going on here: we give mercy and we receive mercy. And this is not coincidental, for the root of the word "mercy" comes from the old Etruscan *merc,* which also gives us "commerce" and "merchant."[5] It's all about exchange.

Usually we think of the mercy of God as a kind of divine clemency, and we pray, "Lord have mercy upon us" as a confession of our weakness and dependency. (Because these qualities are distasteful to a lot of modern people, the "Lord have mercy" prayer has currently gone a bit out of style.) But in this other understanding, mercy is not something God has; it's something that God *is.* Exchange is the very nature of divine life—of consciousness itself, according to modern neurological science—and all things share in the divine life through participation in this dance of giving and receiving. The brilliant young South African teacher Michael Brown writes in his 2005 book *The Presence Process:* "Giving is receiving is the energetic frequency upon which our universe is aligned. All other approaches to energy exchange immediately cause dissonance and disharmony in our life experience." Surely Jesus knew this as well, and his teaching in this beatitude[6] invites us into a deeper trust of that flow. Exchange is at the very heart of his understanding of "no separation."

"Blessed are the pure in heart, for they will see God." This may well be the most important of all the beatitudes—from the perspective of wisdom it certainly is. But what is purity of heart? This is another of those concepts we have distorted badly in our very morality-oriented Christianity of the West. For most people, purity of heart would almost certainly mean being virtuous, particularly in the sexual arena. It would be roughly synonymous with chastity, perhaps even with celibacy. But in wisdom teaching, purity means *singleness,* and the proper translation of this beatitude is, really, "Blessed are those whose heart is not divided" or "whose heart is a unified whole." Remember the *ihidaya*

from chapter 2?—the "single one" who has unified his or her being and become what we would nowadays call "enlightened." According to Jesus, this enlightenment takes place primarily within the heart. When your heart becomes "single"—that is, when it desires one thing only, when it can live in perfect alignment with that resonant field of mutual yearning we called "the righteousness of God," then you "see God." And this does not mean that you see God as an *object* (for that would be the egoic operating system), but rather, you see through the eyes of nonduality; God is the seeing itself.

So this beatitude is not about sexual abstinence; it's about cleansing the lens of perception. The question, of course, is how does one do this? We will be taking up this question in chapter 6, but for now it is worth noting that Jesus flags this particular transformation as the core praxis of the path. Somehow when the heart becomes single, the rest will follow.

"Blessed are the peacemakers, for they will be called the children of God." This beatitude follows as the logical consequence of all that has been laid out so far. When our hearts are gentled and single, when we've tamed the animal instincts, we become peacemakers. We are no longer wielding the sword of the binary operator that divides the world into good guys and bad guys, insiders and outsiders, winning team and losing team. When the field of vision has been unified, the inner being comes to rest, and that inner peaceableness flows into the outer world as harmony and compassion.

"Blessed are those who are persecuted for righteousness' sake, for theirs is the kingdom of heaven." Jesus is not talking about martyrdom here, but about freedom. The Gospel of Thomas records this beatitude with a slight but telling variation that captures the very essence of Jesus's meaning here—and in fact, throughout all the beatitudes:

> Blessed are you in the midst of persecution who,
> When they hate and pursue you even to the core of
>   your being,
> Cannot find "you" anywhere.[7]

Talk about freedom! Whatever this elixir of pure liberation may be, it is what the journey is all about. And it is attained gradually within us—distilled drop by drop from the terror and turmoil of our egoic selfhood—as we learn to let go and entrust ourselves to the Divine Mercy. Situations of persecution (or anything else that shakes us out of our egoic comfort zone) can become great teaching tools if we have the courage to use them that way.

Do the beatitudes appear differently to you against this wisdom backdrop? In these eight familiar sayings we can now see that Jesus is talking about a radical transformation of consciousness, embraced through an attitude of inner receptivity; a willingness to enter the flow; a commitment to domesticate those violent animal programs within us; and above all, a passionate desire to unify the heart. This is a very powerful fourfold path. It has both a contemporaneity and a timelessness to it—not unlike the teaching you would hear today from the Dalai Lama and other great spiritual masters who have dedicated their lives to increasing the quality and quantity of human consciousness.

The Parables

Let's turn now to the parables. Even more so than the beatitudes, these are the familiar and well-loved ground of Jesus's teachings. Who doesn't know the parable of the good Samaritan or the prodigal son? But as I've mentioned already, most of us don't really have a clear idea of what a parable is. We get confused between a parable and a proverb. A proverb is something along the lines of Aesop's Fables: a teaching story with a moral to it, whose purpose is to help us live better and wiser lives. Parables are something completely different—at least the way Jesus uses them. His parables are much closer to what in the Zen tradition would be *koans*—profound paradoxes (riddles, if you like) that are intended to turn the egoic mind upside down and push us into new ways of seeing.

About a generation ago, a few biblical scholars began to catch on to this subversive dimension to Jesus's parables. John Dominic Crossan was one of the first to write on the subject, followed by Bernard Brandon Scott, whose 1989 book *Hear Then the Parable* was widely popularized through its influence on Thomas Keating.[8] These writers all tend to approach the issue of paradox from political and psychological reference points—it has still not been widely seen that what Jesus may really be up to is rewiring our consciousness.[9] but the word is beginning to get out that what we once thought of as beloved folk tales are in fact engaged in some fairly radical sabotage.

Take the good Samaritan, for example, the most famous of all Jesus's parables (you'll find it in Matthew 22:34, Mark 12: 28, and Luke 10:30). If you stick to the surface, it sounds like a cheery little tale about splendid do-gooder. A traveler en route to Jericho runs into trouble on the road; he falls among thieves and is robbed and severely beaten. Two people pass by and decline to get involved. A third arrives and takes pity on the man. He bandages up his wounds, takes him to an inn, pays for his care. This teaching seems to be all about practicing kindness to strangers, and its unsung hero is so manifestly good and generous that we now even have a chain of American recreational vehicle parks named in his honor—the "Good Sam" campgrounds.

What makes this parable so confrontational—and it's easy to miss because the cultural context is no longer obvious—is the fact that the fellow who gets beat up is a Jew, and the fellow who does the rescuing is a Samaritan. Remember the Samaritans? I spoke about them back in the first chapter with regard to the woman at the well. To Jewish eyes, the Samaritans were the despised people, the pariahs. They could do no good, as far as a Jew was concerned. So the subversion begins when the Jew, the chosen person, becomes the victim, and the pariah becomes his rescuer—after two of his own kind have left him for dead. Beneath the cheery surface of this parable Jesus is really forcing the question: "Do you really know as well as you think you do what's good and what's bad? Who are the righteous and who are the not righteous?" It's a direct challenge to that binary operator in the mind, which is so quick to judge, to feel self-meritorious.

We see this same challenge in an even more unsettling way in the parable of the prodigal son (Luke 15:11). Again, this is a familiar story about a younger of two sons who cashes in his inheritance early, squanders the entire sum in riotous living, and then comes home and begs to be taken back in by his father. Remarkably, his father accepts him with open arms and even hosts a grand feast to celebrate his son's return. But the older son is driven absolutely around the bend by this gesture. "How dare you!" he says to his father. "How dare you! My brother has wasted all your money, has made a mockery of you, and now he comes back and you throw a party in his honor. Meanwhile I've been here slaving away for you, and you've offered me nothing. Not a thing—not even a quiet dinner with my friends." And right here is the point of the parable. It's exactly the same point as Jesus was making in the laborers in the vineyard story we looked at earlier. The egoic operating system will always get stuck in judgment and self-meritoriousness. The older brother with his indignant "This isn't fair!" is a textbook example of the egoic operating system at work. Through him, Jesus is asking us to look closely at that part in each one of us that insists on keeping score, that can't let go into the generosity and the blessedness. The parable's concluding image—of the older son standing alone outside, refusing to join the party because he feels he has been slighted—is a vivid symbol of the way the egoic operating system holds us back from joining the dance of Divine Mercy in full swing all around us. If we're stuck in the ego, we can't hear the music.

Once again when we look closely at this parable, we discover that it isn't a sweet little teaching about people doing nice things for other people. It's a challenge to the basic structures, assumptions, and beliefs about ourselves that keep the binary mind firmly in place. It's supposed to challenge you; it's supposed to make you angry—and it's supposed to make you look at yourself more closely. This parable provides particularly rich ground for lectio divina (for specific instructions on how to do this time-tested spiritual practice, look ahead to chapter 13). As you sit with it in meditation, see if you can discover where all

three of these characters—older son, younger son, and father—
live within your own being and what part each one plays in your
life. Allow the parable to become a mirror that reflects back to
you your own state of consciousness. If you work with it that
way, you're using it the way Jesus really intended it, as a tool for
personal transformation of consciousness.

Sometimes Jesus takes the language of paradox and riddle so
far that he leaves people simply scratching their heads. His concepts are always difficult, but sometimes even the words themselves don't make sense. Perhaps the classic example is in the
Gospel of John (3:1), when a Pharisee named Nicodemus comes
to Jesus one night to query him about the spiritual life. Nicodemus is torn in two directions. The small taste of the teaching
he's heard from Jesus clearly intrigues him. But it also unsettles
him, and Jesus has already been flagged as a renegade by Nicodemus's fellow Pharisees. Not wanting to rock the boat publicly,
he slips in under cover of darkness for a private consultation.
Jesus responds to his very gracious initial overture ("Rabbi, we
know you are a teacher who has come from God; for no one can
do these signs that you do apart from the presence of God")
with a completely off-the-wall demand: Nicodemus must be
born again from above, "for unless one person is born again of
water and the Spirit, he cannot inherit the Kingdom of God."
"Wait a minute! This is just too crazy!" gasps poor Nicodemus.
"How can a man go back into his mother's womb and be born
again? What is this man talking about?" Jesus does not roll out
the red carpet for his distinguished visitor. Instead, he throws
him a statement intended to completely destabilize him—essentially the Christian equivalent of the famous Zen koan, "What is
the sound of one hand clapping?"[10]

Once you begin to see it, you can't *not* see it: how this element of subversiveness is the common thread in virtually all
Jesus's teaching. And its principal target is not the Pharisees or
the political situation, but the egoic mind. He is very deliberately trying to short-circuit that grasping, acquiring, clinging,
comparing linear brain and to open up within us a whole new
mode of perception (not what we see, but *how* we see; how the

mind makes its connections). This is a classic strategy of a master of wisdom.

The Hard Teachings

Once you catch the subversive edge in even the more familiar teachings of Jesus, it becomes easier to approach a set of sayings and parables that the church, as a whole, has never quite known how to deal with. They are scattered throughout the four gospels, but you'll find them in their most concentrated dose toward the end of Matthew and the end of Luke. These are the teachings that absolutely refuse to be shochorned into the "Jesus is nice" mold we keep trying to contain him within. One of the thorniest of these is the parable in Matthew 25 about the wise and foolish bridesmaids. As the story opens, a great wedding feast is about to take place, and the ten bridesmaids are waiting for the bridegroom to come. But he is delayed, and they all fall asleep. In the middle of the night they hear the cry, "The bridegroom is coming!" Five of them have remembered to bring oil for their lamps, so they light their lamps and head into the banquet hall. The other five haven't remembered to bring spare oil, and their lamps are now out of fuel. They ask their fellow bridesmaids, "Can we borrow some of your oil so that we can go in to the wedding feast too?" But the five refuse: "If we give you some of our oil, there won't be enough for us. So no thank you; go buy your own." That's the story. And people who try to reconcile it with what they generally take teachings of Jesus to be are left completely stumped.

If Jesus is about sharing, wouldn't it have been nice for the five ladies who had their oil to share it with their friends? How do you make this parable fit with the "blessed are the merciful, for they shall obtain mercy" of the fourth beatitude? At some point the light begins to dawn that Jesus is teaching at a whole different level here; the metaphors work completely differently. These hard teachings are exclusively about inner transformation (not outer actions) and make sense only within that frame of reference. The reason the five bridesmaids who have oil can't give it to the five who don't is that the oil symbolizes something that has to be individually created in you though your own conscious striving. Nobody can give it to you; nobody can take it away from you. The oil stands for the quality of your transformed consciousness, and unfortunately, it's impossible to become conscious unconsciously, through a donation from somebody else. You have to do the work yourself. If you consider the five wise bridesmaids (and hear the word "wise"?) as those who have acquired the "oil" of nondual consciousness, they can't possibly share it with their sisters even if they want to. Their sisters would not be ready yet to receive it.

In the light of this summons to the personal transformation of consciousness, the series of very difficult teachings in Luke also begin to make sense. The series begins in Luke 14:25 with a startling challenge: "Now large crowds were traveling with him; and he turned and said to them, 'Whoever comes to me and does not hate father and mother, wife and children, brother and sister, and even life itself, cannot be my disciple'" (Luke 14:25). What do we make of that? He continues: "For which of you, intending to build a tower, does not sit down first and estimate the cost, to see whether he has enough to complete it? Otherwise, when he has laid a foundation and is not able to finish, all who see it will begin to ridicule him, saying, 'This fellow began to build and was not able to finish.' Or what king, going out to wage war against another king, will not sit down and consider whether he is able with ten thousand to oppose the one who comes against him with twenty thousand?" (Luke 14:28). This teaching seems to say that it's not enough simply to trust in God and throw caution to the winds; we have to be "on top of our game" from the point of view of this world—"wise as serpents, gentle as doves," in another of Jesus's famous teachings. We are not to flee away from the horizontal axis but to *master* it, because only in moving from strength to strength do we really bring forth the Kingdom of Heaven as a reality upon the earth. But he really does mean *master* it, not *be mastered* by it. That's the point of the first saying. "Whoever loves brother and sister more"—that is, if your primary commitments lie entirely along the horizontal axis and you're sentimentally identified with them, you won't find the freedom to seek deeply into this other dimension, which is illumined by the singleness of your heart.

In another difficult teaching (Luke 9:59) a prospective follower asks Jesus, "First may I go home and bury my father?" Jesus's categorical response is, "Let the dead bury their own dead." If you are attached to your identity in this world—if that's the level your consciousness is attuned to—you won't be able to pick up the more subtle frequency he is operating on. You won't be able to follow his lead.

These hard teachings are admittedly disconcerting. You simply can't translate them into a sentimental theology that says, "Jesus just wants us to be nice, to share, to trust." They are classic esoteric teachings, echoed and confirmed throughout the universal wisdom tradition, that speak to the need for a certain spiritual substance (or quality of consciousness) to crystallize in a person before he or she can emerge as a complete human being. But what are these teachings doing here? They are like sophiological tidbits that somehow strayed into our soteriological gospel, and there they stand out like a sore thumb, always irritating and slightly unsettling. And even if the four gospels are all we have to work with, these sayings are odd enough to tweak our suspicion that there might be more to this iceberg of Jesus than meets the eye.

5

A Gospel of Thomas Sampler

THE SUSPICION THAT these difficult sayings of Jesus might actually belong to a different Jesus tradition than anything we're used to in our Christian West received profound confirmation when the Nag Hammadi discovery put the Gospel of Thomas back into general circulation. When this gospel was restored to us (its existence in early Christianity is well attested by the church fathers, but most people assumed it had vanished forever), scholars were at first dubious. "What is this teaching?" they puzzled. "It doesn't make sense!" Because it seemed so different in flavor from what was at the time recognized as "orthodox," the first gambit was to dismiss it as a later, gnostic interpretation of Jesus. But further research kept pointing in the direction that this gospel was early, and that it preserves some of the oldest authentically attested teachings of Jesus. It is most certainly at least as old—if not older—than the four gospels that found their way into the canonical New Testament.[1] What makes Thomas feel so different is that it belongs to the sophiological tradition. It doesn't have any of the biography and narrative you find in the other gospels, and its slant is not toward miracles and healings. It is purely and simply a collection of Jesus's transformational sayings. But as you listen to this gospel in its entirety and allow its paradoxical sayings to slowly sink in, you realize that you are actually gaining a much more complete take on Jesus; you see more clearly where he is coming from—and headed toward. And this expanded picture of his foundational metaphysics confirms that his is indeed, first and foremost, a master of conscious transformation.

The Gospel of Thomas consists of 114 short sayings— or *logia*, as they're known by scholars (*logion* is the Greek term for a saying or aphorism). Virtually all the "hard teachings" from the canonical gospels are represented here—in a context that makes their meaning much easier to grasp—plus a selection of the beatitudes and parables, and many teachings that appear nowhere else. All together, they flesh out the picture of Jesus's teaching, passionately and relentlessly, around the themes of "singleness" and nonduality.

Who wrote it? Was it actually the apostle Thomas, one of the original twelve of Jesus's male disciples, who has gamed fame in our Western tradition as "Doubting Thomas"? This cannot be proved, but Lynn Bauman, who has contributed by far the most thorough and insightful of a recent spate of translations, feels it is certainly plausible, both chronologically and thematically. Thomas is remembered in tradition as the apostle who traveled east to Persia and India, and the teachings in this collection have a distinctly "eastern" feeling to them in their emphasis on the unification of consciousness. Unlike some of the advaitic (nondual) teaching of the East, however, they set forth a vision of wholeness in which this physical plane is neither a mirage nor a trap but rather is an integral part of divine reality with a unique and indispensable role to play. "Singleness" is achieved by mastering that role.

At any rate, tucked away within this enigmatic little gospel are 114 of the most subtle and profound teachings of Jesus—whoever transcribed them was certainly one of his most advanced students. Since this gospel is still fairly unknown terrain for most

Christians, I would like to offer a small sample of its most striking teachings here, together with a very short commentary. All
of these sayings begin with the phrase "Jesus says."[2]

LOGION 7

> Blessed is the lion whom the man devours, for that lion
> will become man. But cursed is the man whom the lion
> devours, for that man shall become lion.[3]

I have referred to this logion already in our discussion of the
third beatitude with regard to the issue of "domesticating" our
animal nature. When the man devours the lion, the animal nature
has been brought under the control of our human reason and
conscious choice. When the lion devours the man, the animal
instincts win out, and that person "devolves" into a lower form.

The teaching here relies on the classic wisdom schematic of
"the great chain of being." As we evolve toward the divine, we
integrate and carry with us the consciousness gained at lower
levels of being. We do not "destroy" or dissolve our lower
nature (images that have so dominated the spiritual journey
in the West); it is not a question of warfare. Rather, we integrate the energy of the animal intelligence so that "lion" gets to
become "man." A part of us does not die so that another part
of us can live. *The whole of us* dies at one level so that *the whole
of us* is reborn at one level. The greatest of the Sufi poets, Jalal-
ludin Rumi (1207–1273), expresses this classic wisdom teaching
in these beautiful lines:

> I died as a mineral and became a plant
> I died as a plant and rose to animal,
> I died as an animal and I was man.
> Why should I fear? When was I less by dying?[4]

It is important to catch the wisdom schematic underlying this
logion: it confirms yet again the lineage that Jesus is working

in and gives us a real taste of the integral nature of the path of transformation he is laying out.

LOGION 22

When you are able
to make two become one,
the inside like the outside,
and the outside like the inside,
the higher like the lower,
so that a man is no longer male,
and a woman, female,
but male and female
become a single whole;
when you are able to fashion
an eye to replace an eye,
and form a hand in place of a hand,
or a foot for a foot,
making one image supercede another
—then you will enter in.

Certainly nondual consciousness has everything to do with being able "to make the two become one." In the first part of this teaching, Jesus describes what the world looks beyond the distortion of that insistent "bifocal lens" of our egoic operating system that mechanically splits our field of perception into paired opposites—inside/outside, male/female, and so forth. This kind of reunification can only happen once we have transcended the egoic operating system; it is in fact synonymous with this transcendence. But what is the result of this unification? The second half of his teaching takes us not into *sunyata*, emptiness (as one might expect in an advaitic or Buddhist teaching), but into an astonishing fecundity. Once one reaches the causal point where all forms converge in oneness (and in this gospel Jesus frequently refers to that point as "the light"), immediately the grand dance of manifestation begins all over again—but this time, you are its master (or at least its conscious servant). I am reminded of a beautiful insight from Jacques Lusseyran, a contemporary philosopher and mystic, whose experience of being blinded in childhood led him straight to that causal point. In the course of long arguments with a musician friend, all of their discussions "ended with an exciting discovery," says Lusseyran: "That there is nothing in the world which cannot be replaced with something else; that sounds and colors are being exchanged endlessly, like the air we breathe and the life it gives us; that nothing is ever isolated or lost; that everything comes from God and returns to God along all the roadways of the world."[5]

Jesus's vision of nonduality certainly begins in Oneness. But it does not stay put there. It dances back and forth between one and two, between "movement and rest" (as he terms it in logion 50), finding its home not in the stasis, but in the dynamism itself.

LOGION 42

Come into being as you pass away.[6]

This shortest of all the logia yet makes a powerful point about the relationship between the horizontal axis and the vertical axis. In the realm of time, we are "passing away." Yet the passage through this realm also gives us the chance to come into being in that other realm; it provides some essential food for the journey if we know how to recognize it and work with it. This is the same theme we met earlier in the parable of the wise and foolish bridesmaids, where the oil for the lamp of consciousness must be distilled "at the intersection of the timeless with time." A few logia later (in 47) Jesus will quote the familiar proverb: "No person drinks aged wine and immediately desires to drink new wine. New wine is not poured into old wineskins, or they might break; an old patch is not sewn onto a new garment for there would be a tear." Time is an indispensable element in the fermenting of that "elixir of being." But only insofar as it is consciously wielded.

LOGION 70

> If you bring forth what is within you, what you have will
> save you. If you do not have that within you, what you
> do not have within you will kill you.

Here again, the accent is on integral development and the bringing into manifestation what would otherwise remain unarticu-
lated. Whatever this spark of consciousness or name of God that
lies at the heart of our being, our role in this human plane is to
bring it into form and fullness. If we fail to do so, it is not just a
failure to germinate: the thing actually turns on us and destroys
us from within. This, incidentally, is exactly the point Jesus is
making in the familiar parable of the talents in the canonical gospels, another of those notoriously "hard teachings" (Matthew
25:14, Mark 4:25, Luke 9:12).

LOGION 77

> I am the light shining upon all things.
> I am the sum of everything,
> For everything has come forth from me,
> and towards me everything unfolds.
> Split a piece of wood, and there I am,
> Pick up a stone and you will find me there.

In this most Zen-like of sayings, Jesus presents himself as the
"suchness"—that quality of pristine awareness underlying and
unifying everything the moment the light of one's awareness
falls on it. This saying also sounds elegantly contemporary: a
vivid description of what some physicists call "the zero-point
field," incorporating dimensions of symmetry, coherence, and
purposiveness. But what gives this saying its poetic power is the
sharp contrast between "macro" and the "micro." "I am the
sum of everything . . ." yet, "Split a piece of wood, and there I
am." A member of our Pacific Northwest Wisdom School took
this logion with him into a work period, and while chopping

wood suddenly experienced the world all around him exploding
energetically into this divine aliveness. Again, it is all one, but the
One expresses itself in the riotous dynamism of the particular.

We also see another allusion here to the great chain of being
I mentioned earlier. Remember Rumi's "I died as a mineral and
became a plant"? The stone and piece of wood remind us of the
pathway of evolution along which all things travel and which
allows Jesus to be present in all created forms by integrating
them into himself.

LOGION 108

> Whoever drinks what flows from my mouth will come
>   to be as I am,
> and I also will come to be as they are,
> so that what is hidden will become manifest.

In this distinctly eucharistic logion, Jesus returns to the idea
of the food chain: the "eating and being eaten" by which we
move from one stage of evolution to another. But here he adds
a shockingly intimate reciprocity to the process. We can certainly understand the first part of this saying: whoever drinks what
flows from the higher will come also to be higher. That's how
the chain works; the lion whom the man devours becomes man.
But what do we make of the second part—"and I also will come
to be as they are"? Does this mean that Jesus is "devolving" to
our own level? No; he is saying something even more radical
than that. Here Jesus leaves even the great chain of being behind
as he steps out into the unknown. In contrast to virtually the
whole salmon-swimming-upstream orientation of the perennial
wisdom—that the way to God is "up," moving from lower to
higher—Jesus here places his entire bet on the process of interabiding: I in you, you in me, all in God, God in all. It is not a ladder but a circle that brings us to God: the continuously renewed
giving and receiving which in its totality is where God dwells.
This kenotic spirituality (self-emptying as the path to fullness)

is in my opinion Jesus's unique and profoundly original contribution to the spiritual consciousness of humankind. We will be exploring it in depth in the next chapter.

Seeing Jesus through this new filter is both profoundly unsettling and profoundly hopeful: unsettling, because it dislodges us even further from our twenty-twenty hindsight—any lingering smugness that we have Jesus's teaching in our hip pocket. But joyous in the sense that our heart knows this already; and profoundly joyous because the spaciousness emerging from this new portrait gives us the freedom to go deeper. I find nothing in the Gospel of Thomas that contradicts any of Jesus's teachings in the canonical gospels. Rather, it rounds them out metaphysically and creates a newfound sense of awe as we see just how original and subtle his understanding really is. He is the first truly integral teacher to appear on this planet. As we take a fresh look at these teachings at once familiar and strange, we're catapulted forward again along a path that rings with the power of truth.

6

Kenosis: The Path of Self-Emptying Love

S O FAR WE have been looking at Jesus as typical of the wisdom tradition from which he comes. An enlightened master recognized by his followers as the Ihidaya, or the Single One, he teaches the art of *metanoia,* or "going into the larger mind." Underlying all his teaching is a clarion call to a radical shift in consciousness: away from the alienation and polarization of the egoic operating system and into the unified field of divine abundance that can be perceived only through the heart.

But how does one make this shift in consciousness? It's one thing to admire it from a distance, but quite another to create it within oneself. This is where spiritual praxis comes into play. "Praxis" means the path, the actual practice you follow to bring about the result that you're yearning for. I think it's fair to say that all of the great spiritual paths lead toward the same center—the emergence of this larger, nondual mind as the seat of personal consciousness—but they get there by different routes. While Jesus is typical of the wisdom tradition in his vision of what a whole and unified human being looks like, the route he lays out for getting there is very different from anything that had ever been seen on the planet up to that point. It is still radical in our own time and definitely the "road less taken" among the various schools of human transformation. I will fill in the pieces of this assertion as I go along, but my hunch is that a good many of the difficulties we sometimes run into trying to make our Christianity work stem from the fact that right from the start people missed how different Jesus's approach really was. By trying to contain this new wine in old wineskins, they inadvertently missed its own distinct flavor. In Jesus everything hangs together around a around a single center of gravity, and you need to know what this center is before you can sense the subtle but cohesive power of the path he is laying out.

What name might we give to this center? The apostle Paul suggests the word *kenosis.* In Greek the verb *kenosein* means "to let go," or "to empty oneself," and this is the word Paul chooses at the key moment in his celebrated teaching in Philippians 2:9–16 in order to describe what "the mind of Christ" is all about. Here is what he has to say:

> Though his state was that of God,
> yet he did not deem equality with God
> something he should cling to.

> Rather, he emptied himself,
> and assuming the state of a slave,
> he was born in human likeness.

> He, being known as one of us,
> humbled himself, obedient unto death,
> even death on the cross.

> For this, God raised him on high
> and bestowed on him the name
> which is above every other name.

So that at the name of Jesus,
every knee should bend
in heaven and on earth and under the earth.

And so every tongue should proclaim
"Jesus Christ is Lord!"
to God the Father's glory.[1]

In this beautiful hymn, Paul recognizes that Jesus had only
one "operational mode." Everything he did, he did by self-
emptying. He emptied himself and descended into human form.
And he emptied himself still further ("even unto death on the
cross") and fell through the bottom to return to the realms of
dominion and glory. In whatever life circumstance, Jesus always
responded with the same motion of self-emptying—or to put it
another way, of the same motion of *descent:* going lower, taking
the lower place, not the higher.

What makes this mode so interesting is that it's almost completely spiritually counterintuitive. For the vast majority of the
world's spiritual seekers, the way to God is "up." Deeply embed-
ded in our religious and spiritual traditions—and most likely in
the human collective unconscious itself—is a kind of compass
that tells us that the spiritual journey is an ascent, not a descent.
Most students of the wisdom tradition consider this upward orientation to be one of the foundational attributes of *sophia perennis* itself, its origins no doubt archetypal.[2] While my own work
with the wisdom Jesus has led me to disagree, it is hard to deny
that the idea of spiritual ascent has been around for a long, long
time. In biblical tradition, the image of the spiritual ladder goes
all the way back to the headwaters of the Old Testament, with
the story of Jacob's dream of the ladder going up to heaven.
It is probably five thousand years old. Christian monastic tradition returned to this image and developed it still further, as
essentially the roadmap for the spiritual journey. The seventh-
century teacher John Climacus ("John of the Ladder") even took
his monastic name from this powerful image, and through his

influential teachings it became the underlying philosophy of monastic practices such as lectio divina and psalmody.³ Ascent mysticism was very much in the air in Jesus's time as well. Earlier in this book I spoke of the Essene community, that apocalyptic Jewish sect whose visionary mysticism and ascetic practices were probably the most immediate formative influence on Jesus. At the heart of the Essene understanding was a particular strain of spiritual yearning known as *merkevah* mysticism. *Merkevah* means "chariot," an allusion to the Old Testament story of the prophet Elijah being taken up to heaven in a chariot. This dramatic episode offered a vivid image of ascent to God, which the Essenes saw as applying both individually and for the entire people of Israel. "The end of the world was at hand," and all eyes were gazing intently upward as Jesus took birth on the earth.

To rise requires energy, in the spiritual realm as well as the physical one. And thus, the vast majority of the world's spiritual technologies work on some variation of the principle of "conservation of energy." Within each person there is seen to reside a sacred energy of being (sometimes known as the "chi," or *prana*, the life force). This energy, in itself infinite, is measured out to each person in a finite amount and bestowed as our basic working capital when we arrive on this planet. The great spiritual traditions have always taught that if we can contain this energy rather than letting it leach away if we can concentrate it, develop it, make it more intentional and powerful—then this concentrated energy will allow us to climb that ladder of spiritual ascent.

This ancient and universal strategy is really at the basis of all genuine asceticism (that is, asceticism in the service of conscious transformation, not as a means of penance or self-mortification). And there is good reason for this: the strategy works. Through the disciplines of prayer, meditation, fasting, and inner witnessing the seeker learns how to purify and concentrate this inner reserve and to avoid squandering it in physical or emotional lust, petty reactions, and ego gratification. As self-mastery is gradually attained, the spiritual energy concentrated within becomes strong enough and clear enough to sustain contact with those increasingly higher and more intense frequencies of the divine life, until at last one converges upon that unitive point. It's a coherent and powerful path of inner transformation. But it's not the only path.

There's another route to center: a more reckless path and extravagant path, which is attained not through storing up that energy or concentrating the life force, but through throwing it all away—or giving it all away. The unitive point is reached not through the concentration of being but through the free squandering of it; not through acquisition or attainment but through self-emptying; not through "up" but through "down." This is the way of kenosis, the revolutionary path that Jesus introduced into the consciousness of the West.

A Pointless Sacrifice?

To flesh out a bit further what this path actually looks like, forgive me if I make a sudden leap into the world of modern literature. Kenosis does not lend itself easily to spiritual theorizing. By far its most powerful and moving enactments have come in the form of story and drama.

One of the most precise descriptions of this path, believe it or not, is the familiar and well-loved story "The Gift of the Magi" by the American author O. Henry. You probably remember the tale. Della and James are newlyweds; they're madly in love with each other. They are also poor as church mice, and their first Christmas together finds them without sufficient funds to buy each other gifts. But each of these lovers does have one prize possession. James owns a gold watch given to him by his grandfather; Della has stunning auburn hair falling all the way to her waist. Unbeknownst to Della, James pawns his gold watch in order to buy her beautiful silver combs for her hair. Unbeknownst to James, Della cuts and sells her hair in order to buy him a gold watch chain. On Christmas eve the two of them stare bewilderedly at their completely useless gifts. It has been a pointless sacrifice—pointless, that is, unless love itself is "the gift of the magi."

And of course, this is exactly what O. Henry is getting at. In the voluntary relinquishing of their most cherished possessions, they make manifest what love really looks like; they give tangible shape to the bond that holds them together. That's what kenosis is all about.

Another profoundly kenotic parable of our times is the tale that forms the 1987 movie *Babette's Feast,* adapted from a short story by Isak Dinesen.[4] As the drama unfolds we discover that its heroine, Babette, had until recently been one of the most celebrated chefs in Paris, but during the political riots of 1871 she loses everything—restaurant, livelihood, and family. She flees for her life to rural Denmark and is taken in by two aging sisters who have given their lives to religious work, trying to hold together the spiritual community that their father founded. When Babette arrives, the remaining believers have grown old and weary, lost in petty bickering. Babette tries as best she can to lift their spirits, but nothing seems to be turning the situation around. Out of the blue a letter arrives informing her that she has won three million francs in a lottery back in Paris, and then and there she decides to treat these Danish peasants to a proper French dinner. She imports all the necessary ingredients: not only exotic gourmet delicacies for the seven-course meal itself (each with its appropriate wines, champagnes, and liqueurs) but the china dinnerware, silver cutlery, damask table cloths, and crystal glassware. The film zerocs in on the banquet table as the astonished Danish peasants are suddenly faced with this extravagant abundance. At first they are frightened and suspicious, but little by little the mood mellows as they slowly relax into gratitude and forgiveness. The last scene of that banquet night has them all stumbling, a bit drunk but very happy, out into the village square, where they form a circle around the fountain (a vivid image in its own right) and begin to sing and dance together. After all these years they have finally touched the wellspring, and their hearts are overflowing. Then someone says to Babette, "Well, I guess you'll be leaving us soon, won't you, now that you're a rich woman?" She says, "Rich? I'm not rich. I spent every penny I had on that banquet, three million francs."

Again we see the same leitmotif as in the O. Henry story. An extravagant sacrifice is in one sense wasted, because these poor peasants cannot really comprehend the magnitude of the gift, and by morning, when they've sobered up, they will probably have lost most of its beneficial effect. But no matter; the banquet table is set before them anyway. In her no-holds-barred generosity Babette offers these broken, dispirited souls a taste of reassurance that their long years of faithfulness have not been in vain. She mirrors to them what God is like, what love is like, what true humanness is like. And she does it precisely by throwing away her entire escape route in a single act of extravagant abundance, extravagant beyond the bounds of earth (and therefore invoking the presence of heaven). That's the kenotic path.

Theologians have sometimes commented that if the goal of ascent mysticism is to bring about union through convergence at the point of origin, the effect of the kenotic path seems to be self-disclosure and new manifestation. The act of self-giving brings new realms into being. It shows what God is like in new and different ways. Some of the most intuitive theologians of our times say that this is how the world was created in the first place—because, in the words of Karl Rahner, "God is the prodigal who squanders himself."[5] The act of self-giving is simultaneously an act of self-communication; it allows something that was coiled and latent to manifest outwardly. "Letting go" (as in nonclinging, or self-emptying) is but a hair's breadth away from "letting be," and our Judeo-Christian tradition remembers that it is through God's original "Let there be . . ." that our visible world tumbled into existence.

The Jesus Trajectory

Love is recklessness, not reason.
Reason seeks a profit.
Loves comes on strong, consuming herself, unabashed.

> Yet in the midst of suffering,
> Love proceeds like a millstone,
> hard-surfaced and straight forward.
>
> Having died to self-interest,
> she risks everything and asks for nothing.
> Love gambles away every gift God bestows.

The words above were written by the great Sufi mystic Jalallu-din Rumi.[6] But better than almost anything in Christian scripture, they closely describe the trajectory that Jesus himself followed in life. He certainly called us to dying to self, but his idea of dying to self was not through inner renunciation or guarding the puri-ty of his being but through radically squandering everything he had and was. John the Baptist's disciples were horrified because he banqueted, drank, and danced. The Pharisees were horrified because he healed on the Sabbath and kept company with women and disreputables, people known to be impure. Boundaries meant nothing to him; he walked right through them.

What seemed disconcerting to nearly everybody was the messy, freewheeling largeness of his spirit. Abundance and a generosity bordering on extravagant seemed to be the signa-tures of both his teaching and his personal style. We have already noted this in two of his parables, where the thing that sticks in people's craws is in each case the display of a generosity so beyond comprehension that it can only be perceived as "unfair." But as we look further, that extravagance is everywhere. When he feeds the multitudes at the Sea of Galilee, there is not merely enough to go around; the leftovers fill twelve baskets. When a woman anoints him with expensive ointment and the disciples grumble about the waste, he affirms, "Truly, I tell you, wherever this good news is proclaimed in the whole world, what she has done will be told in remembrance of her" (Matthew 26:13). He seems not to count the cost; in fact, he specifically forbids count-ing the cost.[7] "Do not store up treasures on earth," he teaches; do not strive or be afraid—"for it is your Father's good pleasure to give you the kingdom" (Luke 12:32). All will come of its own accord in good time and with abundant fullness, so long as one does not attempt to hoard or cling.

It is a path he himself walked to the very end. In the garden of Gethsemane, with his betrayers and accusers massing at the gates, he struggled and anguished but remained true to his course. Do not hoard, do not cling—not even to life itself. Let it go, let it be—"Not my will but yours be done, O Lord. Into your hands I commend my spirit."

Thus he came and thus he went, giving himself fully into life and death, losing himself, squandering himself, "gambling away every gift God bestows." It was not love stored up but love utterly poured out that opened the gates to the Kingdom of Heaven.

Over and over, Jesus lays this path before us. There is nothing to be renounced or resisted. Everything can be embraced, but the catch is to cling to nothing. You let it go. You go through life like a knife goes through a done cake, picking up nothing, clinging to nothing, sticking to nothing. And grounded in that fundamental chastity of your being, you can then throw yourself out, pour yourself out, being able to give it all back, even giving back life itself. That's the kenotic path in a nutshell. Very, very simple. It only costs everything.

Now, I wouldn't say that Jesus was the first or the only teacher in the world ever to have opted for this more reckless and extravagant path, the kenotic way to full union. But it does seem that this was the first time such a teaching had ever been seen in the Near Eastern world, and along with its newness also came confusion. It was a concept so far ahead of its time that even Jesus's closest disciples couldn't quite stay with it. They'd catch it and they'd lose it. Paul catches it exactly in his beautiful kenotic hymn, then loses it in the long lists of rules and moral proscriptions that dominate his epistles. And as the church took shape as an institution, it could not exceed the wingspan of its first apostolic teachers; what they themselves did not fully understand, they could not hope accurately to transmit. Thus, as we will see in the next chapter, right from the start the radical simplicity of Jesus's kenotic path tends to get roped back into the older and

more familiar ascetic models, with a subtle but distinct dissonance that we will be keeping our eyes on.

Dancing the Trinity

Before looking at the long lineage of people who didn't quite
get the path that Jesus was teaching, we need to look briefly at
one group of people who really *did* get it, picking up the torch
that Paul had tossed them in his Philippians hymn and developing it in a powerful and beautiful new way. In Cappadocia in the
fourth century there arose a great contemplative wisdom school
whose guiding lights were Basil of Caesarea, Gregory of Nyssa,
and Gregory of Nazianzus. These three great teachers and profoundly wise beings began to articulate and tease into compre-
hensible form the eternal archetype of the Trinity.[8]

Now the Trinity may be no less confusing than kenosis itself.
Most Christians think of it as "God in three persons"—Father,
Son, and Holy Spirit—and use it primarily to portray their conviction that Jesus is fully divine. (And equally, good Islamic and
Jewish monotheists throw up their hands in dismay, assuming
that Christianity has succumbed to polytheism.) The Cappadocian fathers, however, were not looking at individual persons,
but at the flow of energy between the persons. In fact, the word
we translate as "person" (*hypostasis* in Greek) does not mean an
individual at all, but more a state of being—just as water can
manifest as ice, liquid, or vapor, but remains the same chemical
compound throughout. The Cappadocians were interested in
how this movement, or change of state, takes place. They saw it
as an outpouring of love: from Father to Son, from Son to Spirit,
from Spirit back to Father. And the word used to describe these
mutual outpourings is the same word that we've been looking
at—kenosis.

The Trinity, understood in a wisdom sense, is really an icon of
self-emptying love. The three persons go round and round like
buckets on a watermill, constantly overspilling into one another.
And as they do so, the mill turns and the energy of love becomes

manifest and accessible. The Cappadocians called this complete intercirculation of love *perichoresis,* which literally means "the dance around." Their wonderful and profound insight is that God reveals his own innermost nature through a continuous round dance of self-emptying. On the great watermill of the Trinity, the statement "God is love" brings itself into reality.

After many centuries of highly speculative and abstract scholastic theology, the Trinity is being rediscovered today by some of Christianity's best theologians for what it has essentially been all along—"pure relationality."[9] The brilliant, visionary scholar Raimon Panikkar and the popular Franciscan teacher Richard Rohr have both made it the cornerstone of their own teachings and see it as the tie-rod connecting Christianity not only to its own deepest wisdom but also to the fluid, relational nature of consciousness itself as mirrored in Eastern spiritual thought and in modern quantum physics.[10] You might call it Christianity's yin-yang symbol. It describes how God moves and flows so that love becomes manifest as the unified field of all reality.

The Divine Alchemy

The Trinitarian mystery has immediate implications for us as we try to live Jesus's path. All too often our attempts at self-emptying feel isolated and pointless—"random acts of kindness," as a recent popular bumper sticker puts it. They seem like dead ends, with no real connection to the world at large or even to our own best intentions. Certainly it seemed so in "The Gift of the Magi," when the two newlyweds not only fail to bring off their gift-giving scenarios but inadvertently render each other's heroic sacrifices useless. In *Babette's Feast,* the heroine's profligate generosity also appears to have been largely wasted. What was the final gain in terms of real, permanent, stable change? And the crucifixion: another pointless waste! Why should a good and wise man who could have been a teacher of many die meaninglessly on a cross? Often our own small acts of heroism and sacrifice seem pointless in the same way—except that what the Trinity assures us and what the Cappadocian fathers so perfectly caught is that *no act of kenosis is ever isolated,* no matter how meaningless it looks, no matter how disconnected, no matter how unproductive in terms of reward and gain on this linear axis. Because through the Trinity all kenosis is a tiny hologram of perichoresis. It belongs to that great relational field of "the divine exchange" and connects us instantly with the whole of God, allowing divine love to become manifest in some new and profound dimension. As Raimon Panikkar beautifully expresses it, "I am one with the source insofar as I act as a source by making everything I have received flow again—just like Jesus."[11]

Jesus's teaching assures us as we move toward center along this very reckless and in some ways abundant and extravagant path, not "storing it all up" as in the classic ascetic traditions of attaining being, but "throwing it all away," that divine love is infinite and immediate and will always come to us if we don't cling. This is a powerful statement, so simple and yet so radical that it needs to be ground-truthed again and again in our own lives. But more than just a path, this is also a kind of sacred alchemy. As we practice in daily life, in our acts of compassion, kindness, and self-emptying, both at the level of our doing and even more at the level of our being, something is catalyzed out of that self-emptying which is pure divine substance mirrored in our own true face. Subtle qualities of divine love essential to the well being of this planet are released through our actions and flow out into the world as miracle, healing, and hope.

The power of this sacred alchemy to transform even the blackest of calamity, in which there appears to be absolutely no redemption or saving grace, is attested by an unknown poet who left the following beautiful prayer beside the body of a dead child at the Ravensbrück death camp during a recent era of unspeakable human darkness:

> O Lord, remember not only the men and women
> Of good will, but also those of ill will.

But do not remember all the suffering they inflicted
    on us;
Remember the fruits we have bought, thanks to
This suffering—our comradeship,
Our loyalty, our humility, our courage,
Our generosity, the greatness of heart
Which has grown out of all this, and when
They come to judgment let all the fruits
Which we have borne be their forgiveness.[12]

What an extraordinary testament to the human spirit!
Throughout the entire poem, but particularly in its completely
surprising final word, the divine alchemy is supremely at work,
showing its power to turn even the deepest hardness of cruelty
and atrocity into something new and soft and flowing. And the
template for that alchemy is imprinted in our soul: the Trinitarian impulse which is both the icon of divine reality within us and
the means by which that reality brings itself to fullness. As we
learn not to harden and brace even in the face of what appears
to be ultimate darkness, but to let all things flow in that great
river of kenosis and perichoresis, we come to know—and finally
become—the river itself, which circulates through all things as
the hidden dynamism of love. This, I believe, is the path that
Jesus taught and walked, the path he called us to, the path he
still calls us to.

7

Jesus as Tantric Master

We humans prefer a manageable complexity to an unmanageable simplicity.

—FR. BRUNO BARNHART, OSB CAM.

JESUS'S PATH WAS exactly that, a radically unmanageable simplicity—nothing held back, nothing held onto. It was almost too much for his followers to bear. Even within the gospels themselves, we see a tendency to rope him back in again, to turn his teachings into a manageable complexity. Take his radically simple saying: "Those who would lose their life will find it; and those who would keep it will lose it." Very quickly the gospels add a caveat: "Those who would lose their life *for my sake and the sake of the gospel* will find it." That may be the way you've always heard this teaching, even though most biblical scholars agree that the italicized words are a later addition. But you can see what this little addition has done: it has shifted the ballpark away from the transformation of consciousness (Jesus's original intention) and into martyrdom, a set of sacrificial actions you can perform with your egoic operating system still intact.

Right from the start, the disciples were running for all they were worth keep up with Jesus. The gospels record a comical but poignant trail of miscomprehensions and botched efforts to follow the master's lead, culminating in his near-total abandonment during the crucifixion. And after he left the planet, tendencies set in very early that began to amalgamate his teaching back into the prevailing model of transformation: the upward-tending path of ascent mysticism. At the top of the list was the tendency to portray Jesus as an ascetic and to approach both his teaching and his personal lifestyle from this classic spiritual perspective. As I suggested in the last chapter, I believe that in so doing we have actually blunted the thrust of what Jesus was up to. In a real sense Christianity as a religion got off on the wrong foot from the start.

The problem really boils down to a single word: that *ihidaya* we talked about earlier, a "single one." In a wisdom context this title would be understood to mean an enlightened (or unified) one, a person who had integrated his or her being around the pole of nondual consciousness. But there was no ambient wisdom context at the time, and it did not take long before *ihidaya*, the single one, began to be interpreted in the sense of the single-as-in-celibate: the monk, the classic ascetic, who renounces the entrapments of this world in order to consecrate his life to the higher spiritual pursuits.

Jesus was always a fairly close look-alike for John the Baptist, and in all four gospels the two of them seem to be deliberately paired. The Gospel of Luke portrays John as Jesus's slightly older cousin and contains a delightful passage (Luke 1:44) where the two babies, still *in utero*, recognize and greet each other. We see also that Jesus enters his ministry at the hands of John as John baptizes him in the Jordan River and a voice from heaven announces, "You are my Son, The Beloved" (Luke 3:22). John the Baptist is the archetypal ascetic, most likely an Essene. He looks the part, living alone in the wilderness in his animal skins, feasting on locusts and wild honey, and preaching a message of repentance and inner preparation. Following the classic path of renunciation, he has left behind friends, family, and earthly pleasures in order to dedicate himself entirely to "preparing the way of the Lord."

Superficially Jesus looks like an ascetic as well, but fundamentally he is not. To be sure, he knew the ascetic art form and could do it well when circumstances dictated. All four gospels confirm that immediately after his baptism he entered the wilderness for his forty days of testing and pruning. But what looks like an ascetic from the outside may not prove to be so from the inside. From his subsequent actions we come to understand that Jesus was not so much denying himself earthly food as feasting on the Word of God. He was being formed, inwardly initiated into the radical new path he would soon reveal to the world. When he returned from the wilderness, he did so without any further trappings of renunciation. He moved into the marketplace: taught, healed, laughed and danced and dined; lived among the people as brother and friend. Whatever he learned in the wilderness seems to have pushed him through and beyond the ascetic path.

The reason Jesus and John are paired in the gospels is not to show how they are alike, but to emphasize how they are different. They are intended to be symmetrically paired opposites whose conjunction, like planets in the night sky, is filled with cosmic portent. John himself acknowledges as he baptizes Jesus, "He must increase, but I must decrease" (John 3:30).[1] Symbolically and emblematically, the meaning "for those who have ears" would be that a cosmic cycle has come full term and a new era is about to begin.

Chastity and Celibacy

But Jesus was a celibate, wasn't he? Wasn't he? Isn't this one thing we know for certain? Well, in point of fact, we have no conclusive evidence one way or the other. What we do have is evidence of a lot of tampering with the sources, rewriting of history, and conflation of stories. The picture that emerges to us from the gospels is not necessarily a true picture of what went on—and the picture that emerges from later apostolic and patristic teaching which we commonly call "orthodoxy" is almost certainly a significant distortion of even the scriptures themselves.[2] This incongruity, of course, is the cause of the grass-roots revolution spearheaded by Dan Brown's 2003 novel *The Da Vinci Code,* which attempts to build the case that Jesus was secretly married to Mary Magdalene, that they had a child together, and that the church's attempt to cover up this deep, dark secret has resulted in a two-millennia-long legacy of black-mail, fortune-seeking, and political intrigue.[3]

Here is not the place to jump on the bandwagon with all this sensational, seditious new material. I want to consider the question from a slightly different angle of approach. Why does this new pop mythology have such power to scandalize us? The answer is obvious: because we assume that Jesus was a celibate ascetic and have built our most cherished images of him on the basis of that assumption. If he was secretly sexually active, then he is either a failure or a fraud; either way our house of cards comes tumbling down.

But remember: *ihidaya,* the single one, is not about a state of celibacy but about a fusion of being. It's about becoming single in the sense of mind and heart both going in the same direction, aligned with God, wanting one thing only. This is the singleness that Jesus taught and practiced. Whether or not he did so in a celibate version is not the main point.

If I were to describe the kenotic path he laid out in its broad-est generic terms, using metaphysical rather than theological language, the category that most closely fits is "tantric." Now I know "tantra" is an immediate scare word to a lot of Christians, who think it means making a religion out of having good sex. But "tantra" in its real sense is an ancient and authentic spiritual path, based on a comprehensive metaphysical system. The sym-metrical opposite of the way of the ascetic (or *brahmacharya,* to use the comparable generic name), it seeks the unitive state— that is, the transcendence of separation and duality—through a complete self-emptying or self-outpouring. Sexual expression can indeed be a facet of this self-outpouring, but it is by no means the tail wagging the dog. If you recall our discussion of the kenotic path from the last chapter, I think you'll agree that the word "tantra" at least puts us in the ballpark of what Jesus was talking about, much more so than the ascetic path of storing up and renouncing.

There is a slight but crucial difference in flavor between renunciation and letting go. In renunciation you push things away from you; you say "no" and hold yourself a bit apart from them so that they don't contaminate you or deflect you from your aim. In the kenotic or tantric path, anything can come toward you, and you can embrace it fully; you preserve your chastity simply by not clinging. In the free flow of this coming and going (which as we saw in the last chapter belongs to the perichoresis, or "dance around," of divine love) you dwell in safety.

Chastity is certainly a requirement of the kenotic path, but chastity is not the same thing as celibacy nor is it necessarily preserved by celibacy. A charming story from the Buddhist tradition makes the distinction quite clear. Two monks are traveling together, both of them sworn to a strict celibacy that proscribes any interaction whatsoever with the opposite sex. They come to a deep river and see a woman standing beside it, obviously desperate to get across but unable to swim. One of the monks simply slings her up on his back and swims her across. When they reach the other side, the woman goes on her way and the monks continue on theirs. Two hours later the first monk notices that his brother is silently fuming. "How could you have done that?" the second finally explodes. "You are under vows never to touch a woman. Do your vows mean nothing to you? Don't you care that you have contaminated yourself?" "My brother," replies the first, "I picked her up and put her down. You're still carrying her."

We can say with categorical certainty that Jesus practiced a path of chastity, of full singleness and purity of heart. He embraced everyone and everything but took nothing to himself for his own profit. People were not manipulated; they did not become fodder for his spiritual ambitions or his animal instincts. And when it was time to let go, he did so with the same equanimity and freedom he had shown in the original embrace.

Chaste he definitely was. He is virtually the archetype of chastity. But whether that involved a dimension of physical celibacy, we simply do not know.

But why should this be such an all-important issue? Why should Dan Brown's *Da Vinci Code* and other works riding its wave make millions exposing the church's "deep, dark, secret"? The underlying issue here is actually far more explosive than the surface uproar. For the fact remains that *celibacy is an essential requirement of the ascetic path but not of the kenotic one.* The church's insistence on Jesus's celibacy and its defensive hysteria around the suggestion that this may not in fact be so are merely further evidence that from the start Christianity has gotten the Jesus path slightly wrong. If we truly recognized him for what he was, his relationship with a human beloved would be a cause for joy, not consternation. If for nothing else, we owe *The Da Vinci Code* a profound debt of gratitude for exposing where all along the root of the problem has lain.

Will the Real Mary Magdalene Please Stand Up?

So were they in fact human beloveds? Who is this Mary Magdalene anyway? These questions are in the foreground of people's attention today. The canonical gospels are unanimous in their testimony that she was the first witness to Jesus's resurrection and virtually unanimous that she was also steadfastly present throughout the entire crucifixion and burial (a fact curiously deemphasized in the Holy Week liturgy).[4] Beyond this, they have little else to say about her, but the new material emerging from Nag Hammadi and parallel discoveries is augmenting the picture considerably. She has a significant voice in the Gospel of Thomas. She also figures prominently in the Gospel of Philip and the Gospel of Mary Magdalene, and these three texts go a long way toward correcting the errors of omission and commission that have accumulated in Christian tradition, particularly in the Christian West.

Traditionally she has been portrayed in the West as a repentant prostitute from whom Jesus cast out seven demons. But scholars have conclusively demonstrated that this picture of her is a medieval fabrication, largely attributable to the sixth-century theologian and pope St. Gregory the Great. What we do know now is that Mary Magdalene was almost certainly a full-fledged disciple of Jesus and quite likely his most advanced student. This statement in itself is challenging to the status quo, because many people will still insist that Jesus only had male disciples. (As a matter of fact, there's a whole line of theological argument that tries to bar women from the priesthood by saying that since all Jesus's disciples were male, only males can be priests.) But the evidence emerging both from these new texts and from the canonical gospels themselves (if you read between the lines) is that this simply wasn't so. Jesus's band of close followers included both men and women, and the women were not merely camp followers or support staff. He taught them and had enjoyed their fellowship; they were his intimates, Mary Magdalene most of all.

Many people believe that Mary Magdalene is identical with Mary of Bethany (of Mary, Martha, and Lazarus fame), with whom Jesus enjoyed a personal friendship and evidently spent a considerable amount of his free time. (One feminist scholar, Margaret Starbird, suggests that the "Magdalene" part of her name does not refer to the town of Magdala at all, but is actually a nickname—"Mary the Tower"—used within Jesus's intimate group of disciples to denote the stature she held among them.[5]) The whole question remains highly speculative, but what is certain—implicit in the canonical gospels and lucidly clear in the Gospel of Mary Magdalene and the Gospel of Thomas—is that Mary was right there sitting at Jesus's feet and that she got the message. She got it better than the others, and this created tension among the disciples, particularly between herself and Peter.

The canonical gospels tend to downplay conflict among the disciples;[6] their approach to resolving the apparent tension between Mary Magdalene and the male disciples is simply to silence her voice. But both the Gospel of Mary Magdalene and the Gospel of Thomas make no attempt to hide the fact that this tension exists, and they are candid about the reasons for it. In the following extract from the Gospel of Mary Magdalene, the simmering conflict comes spilling out:

> Andrew's response was to say to the rest of the brothers: "Say what you will about all that she has said to us, I for one do not believe that the Savior said such things to her, for they are strange and appear to differ from the rest of his teachings." After consideration, Peter's response was similar: "Would the Savior speak these things to a woman in private without openly sharing them so that we too might hear? Should we listen to her at all, and did he choose her over us because she is more worthy than we are?" Then Mary began to weep, saying to Peter: "My brother, what are you thinking? Do you imagine that I have made these things up myself within my heart, or that I am lying about the Savior?" Speaking to Peter, Levi also answered him: "You have always been quick to anger, Peter, and now you are questioning her in exactly that same manner, treating this woman as if she were an enemy. If the Savior considered her worthy, who are you to reject her? He knew her completely and loved her faithfully."[7]

Andrew's outburst was precipitated by a lengthy discourse from Mary Magdalene explaining a private teaching she had received from Jesus (most likely through a vision sometime before the resurrection) about the struggle to tame the inner passions and break free into full unitive consciousness. While unfortunately less than half of this dialogue still survives (four pages of the original manuscript are missing at this point), its final lines reveal a depth and poetic beauty that rivals anything in canonical scripture:

> And my soul sang: "What has bound me has been slain. What encompassed me has been vanquished. Desire has reached its end, and I am freed from Ignorance. I left

one world behind with the aid of another, and now as Image I have been freed from the analog. I am liberated from the chains of forgetfulness which have existed in time. From this moment onward I go forward into the fullness beyond time, and there, where time rests in the stillness of Eternity, I will repose in silence."[8]

This beautiful quotation exposes what was no doubt at the heart of the conflict: Mary, more than any of the other disciples, caught the incredible subtlety of what Jesus was teaching. She saw that he really did come from another realm of being and that his purpose was to make that realm manifest here and now. She also had a strong personal taste of its atmosphere: its timelessness and the clarity of eternal remembrance (that is, pure consciousness) once the passions have been brought under control. She was able to penetrate into his integral, nondual vision of wholeness. And that was absolutely galling to the other apostles, particularly to Peter, who had a much more traditionally Jewish view of the place of women in spiritual groups, which was certainly not right at the feet of the Master.

The conflict again breaks out in full force in the final logion of the Gospel of Thomas, as Peter announces abruptly, "Mary should leave us, for women are not worthy of this life." Jesus's reply is curious:

> Then I myself will lead her
> Making her male if she must become
> Worthy like you males!
> I will transform her into a living spirit
> Because any woman changed in this way
> Will enter the divine realm.[9]

This response has caused considerable unnecessary distress to many feminists, who hear him saying that a woman must turn into a man before she can enter the kingdom (indeed, the "place of last scholarly resort" has sometimes been invoked: trying to dismiss this logion as a spurious later addition). But the key to

the riddle lies in logion 22 ("When you are able to fashion an
eye to replace an eye, and form a hand in place of a hand, or a
foot for a foot, making one image supercede another—then you
will enter in"; see the discussion of this logion in chapter 5 to
refresh yourself), plus Jesus's highly developed sense of irony,
visible throughout this entire gospel. He is not saying that Mary
must become a male; he is saying that Peter must grow beyond
his egoic mind. To offer a contemporary paraphrase, he replies,
"If it's so all-fired important to you guys trapped in your binary
reality to have her be male—poof! We'll make her male. What's
the big deal? It's simply one image superceding another." Then
he turns to his real point: "I will transform her into a living spirit." A living spirit—and remember this is the final teaching in
the Gospel of Thomas, summing up everything that has gone
before—is one who has transcended the categories, that insistent male/female, right/wrong, "one of us"/"not one of us"
egoic protocol. He concludes, "Any woman changed in this way
[that is, into a living spirit] will enter the divine realm." You can
read between the lines and conclude that any man changed in
this way will enter the divine realm as well.

What Jesus is saying here, powerfully and clearly, is that if you
do the work of transforming your being, moving beyond the
egoic mind, then you become a living spirit. For Jesus, Mary
Magdalene was clearly a living spirit. Theirs was a passionate
soul-love, but it was founded in the nondual, not in egoic
drama. She had attained to his level of perception; she could
see the Kingdom of Heaven with her own eyes and walk it on
her own two feet. This is why she was able to stand firm during
the crucifixion and burial when the other disciples were fleeing for
their lives and why, according to the Gospel of Mary Magdalene,
she was able to rally the terrified disciples with her words of
reassurance: "Do not weep and grieve or let your hearts remain
in doubt, for his grace will be with you all, sustaining and
protecting you."[10] She had completely integrated what Jesus
was about.

Easter Morning

Long before I became a priest, I worked as a professional medieval dramatist. For many years during the Easter season I would stage one of the beautiful medieval resurrection plays, which always conclude with the touching scene between Jesus and Mary Magdalene recorded in John 20:11–18. As a director, I had to understand what motivated these characters, what made them tick. And on this score there could be no doubt: it was love, pure and simple. Mary Magdalene arrives at the tomb on Easter morning intently focused on her purpose. She has at this point stood vigil for three days, and nothing is left of her except pure yearning. She refuses to be dissuaded by angels who tell her that Jesus is risen (but gone somewhere else); she will accept nothing less than his presence, even if the closest she can come to it is to gaze one last time upon his beloved body. "Please, sir," she implores a man whom she takes to be the gardener, "if you have taken him away, tell me where you have put him, and I will go remove him." And finally Jesus speaks to her, calling her by name, and she recognizes him and throws herself at his feet with the ecstatic cry, "Rabboni! [My master!]" Easter Sunday begins with the energy of this encounter; it reverberates with two hearts reunited, her yearning met in his response. At the epicenter of what Christians call "the Easter kerygma" (the proclamation of the good news of the resurrection) is a powerful moment of pure love.

The very next words he says to her have long puzzled both scholars and believers alike, but in the light of the path we have been exploring in this book, they become crystal clear. "Do not cling to me, for I have not yet ascended to my father." He is reminding her of the kenotic path. Yes, theirs is a pure love, but it will henceforward be expressed in a new form. Don't cling. Rather, go forth and announce the good news to the disciples.

On the basis of this charge given to her by Jesus himself, Mary Magdalene has traditionally been known in the church as "apostle to the apostles" (even though the dilemma of why the "apostle to the apostles" is not herself an apostle has never been satisfactorily resolved). The gospel narratives unanimously leave us with a powerful icon of the deep and pure soul love between Jesus and Mary Madgalene and attest that it is on the basis of this love that she is able to proclaim the resurrection as a living reality. Clearly a very deep mystical bond between the two of them, stronger than physical life and death, becomes profoundly engendering to the whole subsequent unfolding of Christianity. In a sense—and without wanting to make unfair distinctions— one must honestly say that the Christian path was not founded by the male disciples, although they are given the credit for it. It grew heart and soul out of the pure love and trust between a man and a woman who had, in a deep way, transcended their male- and female-ness to become living spirits.

A Church of Love

Of course, it is not hard to see what happened next; the seeds are already implicit in the canonical gospels and right in your face in the Gospels of Thomas and Mary Magdalene. This kind of a love relationship, embracing both soul and spirit in a complete trans- formation of being, was far beyond the pale of what Peter or any of the other disciples could fathom. It broke every norm they were familiar with. Even in the Gospel of Matthew (19:6), when Jesus teaches that man and wife are to become "one flesh," the disciples roll their eyes and say, "This is too hard! It would be better not to marry!" If the laying down of self is hard enough to bring off individually, imagine doing it as a couple! Peter and his cohorts simply couldn't make the leap. (And Paul, who was never part of the day-to-day interactions of Jesus's inner circle and most likely never met Mary Magdalene, couldn't even con- ceive that the leap existed.) By the time of the earliest Christian writings, then, we can already see a kind of artful dissembling setting in. The assumption begins to take root that Jesus was a celibate and that the way one most closely follows his path is to embrace that state oneself.

Where does this leave us twenty centuries later? Again let me say that the issue of Jesus's sexual expression (or lack thereof) is of no personal concern to me. What does concern me is that over the centuries the Church, in its growing discomfort with sexuality, has also inadvertently become afraid of love, retreating from the very heart of Jesus's kenotic path. By the fourth century, celibates had emerged as a privileged caste within Christianity (to enter the power structure as a priest, bishop, abbot, or theologian required a vow of celibacy)—in fact, for the better part of two millennia Christian theology has been entirely framed within the context of celibates talking to other celibates. There are beautiful words spoken and powerful insights shared, but implicitly a whole walk of human experience is devalued. Celibate theology tends to reinforce the message that to love God utterly, one must renounce human partnership and be wary of any romantic entanglements that might "divide the heart."[11] If you choose to walk the path of committed relationship with a partner, somehow there's a sense that religiously you are a second-class citizen, incapable of the highest level of spiritual commitment. At very least, sexual expression (which is a lower state of "purity" than celibacy) needs to be carefully managed, and redeemed insofar as possible by being consecrated to procreation.

But Jesus didn't say that. He didn't teach that. Perhaps the fundamental flaw in the argument is to picture God as an object in the first place, a "someone" or "something" that you can love all the way. God is never the object of love. That's just another example of the egoic operating system splitting the field of perception. God is always and only the *subject* of love, flowing through our relationships, through our opportunities and also our challenges, through each and every one of the particular conditions we find ourselves in at any given moment. No one and nothing is excluded. As Jesus so profoundly stated in that final logion of the Gospel of Thomas, it is not a matter of whether you're male or female, celibate or sexually active, a monk or married. What matters is that you become a living spirit. And a living spirit is a person who, like Jesus, has become *ihidaya,* who has moved beyond the opposites. We do this in life wherever we find ourselves. Men do it, women do it, couples do it, monks do it. Anyone who is willing to take up the burden of the much more difficult task—not the manageable complexity of rules and regulations, but the unmanageable simplicity of being present to your life in love—that person is walking the path of Jesus.

PART TWO

The Mysteries of Jesus

8

The Incarnation

Time held me green and dying,
though I sang in my chains like the sea.

— DYLAN THOMAS, "FERN HILL"

I N THE FIRST PART of this book we explored Jesus's teachings as a comprehensive spiritual path. In this second part we will be shifting our focus to consider Jesus's life itself as a teaching. By "a teaching" I mean a model, of course; all authentic teachers walk the talk. But more than just a model, I want to consider his life as a *sacrament*—that is, as a spiritual force in its own right. The traditional definition of a sacrament is "an outward and visible sign of an inward and spiritual grace."[1] But what to my mind this definition does not make sufficiently clear is that a sacrament does not merely *symbolize* a spiritual reality; it lives that reality into existence.

Jesus's life, considered from this standpoint, is a sacrament: a mystery that draws us deeply into itself and, when rightly approached, conveys an actual spiritual energy empowering us to follow the path that his teachings have laid out. This sacramental life of Jesus rests on four cornerstones which are both historical events and cosmic realities: his incarnation, passion, resurrection, and ascension. Together they compose the foundation of the Christian mystical and devotional life, and to open oneself fully to the meaning of these great mysteries is to be able to read the inner roadmap of the Christian path. In the next four chapters we will be exploring each of these mysteries in turn. My hope is to move beyond the usual theological and critical-historical explanations in order to follow the living mystical thread that will allow us to appropriate each one of these mysteries as food for the journey.

Since the ground we will be traversing is also the sometimes prickly shared territory of Christian liturgy and sacramental theology, let me remind you once again of my own background here, so that you will know where I am speaking from. While I wear the collar of an Episcopal priest, most of my lived liturgical life has been within the wider stream of Benedictine monasticism, primarily Western and Roman Catholic (although the Episcopal liturgy is in most respects identical), and it is from this perspective (as well as my earlier training as a medievalist) that I will primarily be speaking when I describe the ritual celebrations that unfold these great mysteries. I am less familiar with the Orthodox traditions (except through my exposure to the Christian inner tradition), but at ease within the Celtic and Oriental Orthodox spiritual streams, whose extraordinary insights I will draw on at appropriate moments. As Meister Eckhart once observed, "There is no being except in a mode of being," and the Western Catholic mode of being is the stream in which I have primarily come to know what I know. With that disclaimer in place, let us see what we can discover about the first great mystery, the incarnation.

"For God So Loved the World . . ."

I remember being struck many years ago by an insight from the contemporary mystic Bernadette Roberts that crucifixion wasn't really the hard thing for Jesus; the hard thing was incarnation.[2] Crucifixion and what followed from it—his death and resurrection—were simply the pathway along which infinite consciousness could return to its natural state. What was really hard for infinite consciousness was to come into the finite world in the first place. With nothing to gain from the human adventure—nothing to prove, nothing to achieve, and a dangerously unboundaried heart that left him defenseless against the hard edges of this world—Jesus came anyway: that, claims Bernadette Roberts, was the real crucifixion! As we saw earlier, Paul grasped that same point in his beautiful hymn in Philippians 2:9–16. The first self-emptying that Jesus goes through is the self-emptying that lands him in bodily form on this planet, a human being. There is definitely something spiritually counterintuitive about this business of incarnation, and to really get what's at stake in this mystery is for me the acid test as to whether you understand what Christianity is all about.

Unfortunately, this understanding is hard to come by: not only outside of Christianity, but inside it as well.

Make no mistake—Christianity is intensely a religion of incarnation. Millions of people caught up in mass hysteria during the Christmas season can't *all* be wrong! But even the sentimental excesses of the season only go to reinforce the point. There is a deeper truth at work here that stirs us in spite of ourselves. Who among us has not awakened in the wee hours of Christmas morning to catch the live broadcast of the Ceremony of Lessons and Carols from Westminster Abbey and thrilled to the sonorous reading of those immortal words from the prologue to the Gospel of John: "In the beginning was the Word, and the Word was with God, and the Word was God . . . And the Word became flesh and dwelled among us"? There is a deep soul-truth here that both contains and redeems our frantic efforts to penetrate its meaning at a more superficial level.

If you were to imagine the great world religions like the colors of a rainbow, each one witnessing in a particular way to some essential aspect of the divine fullness, Christianity would unquestionably hold down the corner of incarnation—by which I mean

the vision of God in full solidarity with the created world, fully
at home within the conditions of finitude, so that form itself
poses no impediment to divinity. There is another beautiful
phrase in John's gospel proclaiming: "For God so loved the
world that He gave His only Son" (John 3:16). At its mystical
best, Christianity reverberates with the warmth of this assurance: with the conviction that creation is good, that God is for
us, and that what ultimately gets worked out in the sacred mystery of Jesus's passage through the human realm is a profound
testament to love.

Who Screwed Up?

Unfortunately, Christianity as a religion has never had a sufficient metaphysical understanding of its own core truth. The
message gets obscured by its primary interpretive vehicle: the
theology of fall and redemption. Virtually all Christian teaching
begins from the supposition that Jesus's incarnation is brought
about by the fall of Adam and happens in response to it. "As in
Adam all died, so in Christ shall all be made alive" is the classic Pauline formulation of this idea (1 Corinthians 15:20). The
primordial parents Adam and Eve ate the forbidden fruit and
plunged the world into chaos; Jesus came to rescue it. Thus,
incarnation is framed from the start within the context of God's
response to a mistake that should never have happened in the
first place. This assumption, in turn, deeply colors our understanding of the phrase, "For God so loved the world that he
gave his only Son." It sounds like: "God didn't give up on us;
God bailed us out."

In a more mystical nuancing of this same basic idea, we
encounter the theology of "O felix culpa"—"O happy fault"—
to quote the first line of a traditional Gregorian Advent hymn
which expresses this theology particularly clearly. Rather than
blaming Adam and Eve, this line of argument claims, we ought
to be grateful for them because their mistake set in motion the

chain of events through which Christ would fully reveal himself
to this world. Without that initial fall there would have been
no need for the redemption. In the most subtle versions of this
teaching (as in Karl Barth's *Christ and Adam*[3]) linear cause and
effect are reversed, and we see Adam and Eve falling into this
space/time continuum out of God's "prior" decision (that is,
already made in eternity) to reveal himself in human form. Rather than being the cause of the fall, Adam and Eve become the
instruments of the ultimate divine self-communication. This is
a much more affirmative teaching, which brings the theology of
fall and redemption to its most mature expression.

But I would like to push the metaphysical envelope still
further and see if we can approach the mystery of the incarnation through a conceptual framework that does not rely on fall
and redemption at all but unfolds along an entirely different
line of understanding. Instead of a cosmic course-correction,
this other approach envisions the steady and increasingly intimate revelation of divine love along a trajectory that was
there from the beginning. The best expression of this idea is
actually contained in a beautiful saying from Islamic tradition
(although its roots go down into perennial wisdom ground):
"I was a hidden treasure, and I loved to be known, and so I
created the worlds both visible and invisible."[4] Both the saying
itself and the understanding that illumines it derive from a
profound mystical intuition that our created universe is a vast
mirror, or ornament (and the Greek word "cosmos" literally
means "an ornament"), through which divine potentiality—
beautiful, fathomless, endlessly creative—projects itself into
form in order to realize fully the depths of divine love. And
remember that "realize" has two meanings: "to recognize" and
"to make real." The act of loving brings hidden potential to full
expression, and the more intimate and costly the self-giving,
the more precious the quality of love revealed. This subtle and
beautiful understanding of creation will also, as we shall see,
have something very important to show us about our true work
as human beings.

"Many Dwelling Places"

We Christians still inhabit a rather small universe, metaphysically speaking. We know that we live here on earth, and some of us may believe that above it is a place called heaven, counterbalanced by a place down below called hell. At very best it's a three-tiered universe. But the ancient wisdom traditions (now strongly reinforced, incidentally, by findings emerging from modern physics and cosmology) universally suggest that we need to throw this three-story world out; it is far too cramped to contain the vastness of divine consciousness. There are many realms, wisdom teaches: not just earth, heaven, and hell, but countless densities or dimensions of existence, all of which exist to manifest or mirror an aspect of the divine fullness. Jesus himself states this very clearly to the disciples in his farewell discourses in the Gospel of John, when he says, "In my Father's house there are many dwelling places" (John 14:2). He does not mean physical places but rather states of consciousness or dimensions of divine energy (as we saw in chapter 3 with Jim Marion's recognition that the "Kingdom of Heaven" was Jesus's way of referring to nondual consciousness). The tradition of *sophia perennis* (perennial wisdom) pictures this vastness as a "great chain of being" or "ray of creation,"[5] which begins in a pure, high-intensity, invisible, subtle consciousness and "descends," thickening as it does so, into this world we inhabit: the realm of sharp edges and tables and chairs and human beings crashing and banging against each other in a finite and terribly solid world.

The contemporary Christian hermeticist Valentin Tomberg envisions this ray as a vast energetic cascade, beginning in divine consciousness itself and ending up in our familiar empirical universe. In *Meditations on the Tarot* he writes: "Modern science has come to understand that matter is only condensed energy. Sooner or later science will also discover that what it calls energy is only condensed psychic force, which discovery will lead in the end to the establishment of the fact that all psychic force is the condensation, purely and simply, of consciousness; i.e., spirit."[6]

Like a mountain whose base is solidly on the earth but whose summit is hidden in the clouds, this insight leads us step by step up the ray of creation. Modern physics certainly would have no difficulty with the assertion that matter is only condensed energy; this is officially the Second Law of Thermodynamics. But what about this next realm, "psychic force"? Here the paths divide. This second form of energy is well known to spiritual seekers, but largely invisible to hardcore science; it is the energy flowing through prayer, attention, intention, and will: those more subtle exchanges which science has so far declined to measure but which we know have the power to create demonstrable effects in the physical realm.[7]

Beyond psychic force, yet another energetic realm awaits us, claims Tomberg, for psychic force is itself only the "condensation" (that is, the densification or coarser expression) of a substance incomparably more intense and subtle: pure spirit, pristine consciousness itself, unmediated by any form of expression. This primordial quality is known by many names in the tradition—"I AM" in Judeo-Christian tradition, *wujud* ("reality") in mystical Islam, *rigpa* ("pristine awareness") in Tibetan Buddhism. The names vary, but the understanding remains the same. Virtually unanimously, the ancient wisdom roadmaps picture the cosmos as a vast light stream, radiating out from the ineffable Godhead through the realm of primordial intention (known in Christianity as the *logos*), into archetypal form and energies, and finally into human, earthly becoming. Our life here in this physical cosmos is merely the endpoint of a long journey of what you might call "divine redshift"—that is, the condensation or cooling down of the intense energy of pure spirit in order to make physical manifestation possible.[8]

Down Here on the Edge

So here we find ourselves on this plane of existence, at or near the bottom of the great chain of being. What are we to make of our position? What are we doing "down" here in a world that seems so dense and sluggish, so coarse and fragile and finite? Even in our dreams we move faster than the speed of light, and our mystics and visionaries are perpetually reminding us that in our heart of hearts we remember and yearn for a state of greater spaciousness and fluidity.

It's curious, when you come to think about it, how virtually all the world's spiritual traditions see this earthly realm as somehow deficient. Depending on the tradition, our world is either an illusion or a mistake, but in either case we "fall" into it, from a lighter gravitational field to a heavier one. We have seen how the Judeo-Christian tradition upholds this understanding in its primordial myth of the fall of Adam and Eve. Other traditions (primarily the Eastern ones) see this world as a mirage, an illusion to be dispelled. Still other traditions, such as mystical Islam, carry a profound sense of exile and a "nostalgia for the infinite." Here is not home.

Is there another way of looking at this? I believe there is, and I think that it is actually at the heart of what is intended by that beautiful mantra, "For God so loved the world that he gave his only Son." But it is so spiritually counterintuitive that it remains almost entirely unspoken—at least I myself have never heard it spoken or written about in any of the traditions. To the extent that what I am seeing here is correct, Christian wisdom steps out into unknown territory, leaving even *sophia perennis* behind.

Here is my take:

Yes, this is a very heavy, frustrating, difficult density that we come into by taking birth in the human realm. Because of the binary, finite nature of both the physical world itself and the egoic operating system we use to navigate it, it seems as though we're always bumping into sharp edges. Life presents us with a series of seemingly irrevocable choices: to do one thing means that we have to give up something else; to marry one person means we can't marry another; and to join a monastery means we can't marry at all. Our confused agendas clash both inwardly and outwardly, and we cause each other pain. Our bodies age; we diminish physically; loved ones fall out of our lives. And the force of gravity is tenacious, nailing our feet to the ground and usually our souls as well. I remember my granddaughter, now five, who from the very moment she arrived on this planet experienced an intense frustration bordering on fury at her inability to move. "What the hell?" she seemed to be saying as she flailed her little arms and legs and tried even at four months old to wriggle herself across the room. I have never seen a child who felt the constriction of this planet as much as she did.

Yes, we come into constriction, but is that the same as punishment? I believe not. I believe rather that this constriction is a *sacrament,* and we have been offered a divine invitation to participate in it.

Remember our discussion of sacrament at the beginning of this chapter? A sacrament reveals a mystery in a particularly intense way while at the same time offering the means for its actualization. And in this sphere of human life, the sacrament is finitude and the mystery is "I was a hidden treasure and I loved to be known . . ."

Notice that there is a subtle double meaning at work in this phrase. At one level "I loved to be known" is a synonym for "I longed to be known" (and the phrase is often translated that way). But you can read the words in another way—"I loved *in order to* be known"—and when you do, they reveal a deeper spiritual truth. In order to become known to another, we must take the risk of loving that person, and this includes the real possibility of rejection and the even more painful prospect of heartbreak if the beloved is lost to us. It is difficult to risk love in a world so fragile and contingent. And yet, the greater the gamble of self-disclosure, the more powerful the intimacy and the more profound the quality of devotion revealed.

Could it be like this for God as well?

Could it be that this earthly realm, not in spite of but *because of* its very density and jagged edges, offers precisely the conditions for the expression of certain aspects of divine love that could become real in no other way? This world does indeed show forth what love is like in a particularly intense and costly way. But when we look at this process more deeply, we can see that those sharp edges we experience as constriction at the same time call forth some of the most exquisite dimensions of love, which require the condition of finitude in order to make sense—qualities such as steadfastness, tenderness, commitment, forbearance, fidelity, and forgiveness. These mature and subtle flavors of love have no real context in a realm where there are no edges and boundaries, where all just flows. But when you run up against the hard edge and have to stand true to love anyway, what emerges is a most precious taste of pure divine love. God has spoken his most intimate name.

Let me be very clear here. I am not saying that suffering exists in order for God to reveal himself. I am only saying that *where* suffering exists and is consciously accepted, *there* divine love shines forth brightly. Unfortunately, linear cause-and-effect has progressively less meaning as we approach the deep mysteries (which originate beyond time and thus have no real use for it). But the principle can be tested. Pay attention to the quality of human character that emerges from constriction accepted with conscious forgiveness as compared to what emerges from rage and violence and draw your own conclusions.

At any rate, I have often suspected that the most profound product of this world is tears. I don't mean that to be morbid. Rather, I mean that tears express that vulnerability in which we can endure having our heart broken and go right on loving. In the tears flows a sweetness not of our own making, which has been known in our tradition as the Divine Mercy. Our jagged and hard-edged earth plane is the realm in which this mercy is the most deeply, excruciatingly, and beautifully released. That's our business down here. That's what we're here for.

Unveiling Love

If my hunch is correct, you can see how it significantly rear-ranges the playing field. Our earthly existence, then, is not about good behavior in preparation for a final judgment. It's not a finishing school in which we "learn what we need to learn," nor a sweatshop in which we work off our karmic debt. Right here and now we are in the process of speaking into being the revelation of God's most hidden and intimate name. That's a difficult assignment, particularly when "success" and "failure" mostly wind up being the complete opposites of what we would normally expect in life. But the most productive orientation for our time here is not to focus on how quickly we can get back to our spiritual homeland, but to give ourselves fully to the divine intimacy being ventured right here and now. We might reassure ourselves that in some conscious (or deeply trans-conscious) way, we have chosen to bear our part in what mystical tradition calls "the suffering of God": the costliness that is always involved in the full manifestation of divine love. We're doing it here and now, through the marrow of our own human lives, consciously lived. And these space-time conditions, as fragile and as frustrating as they are, are precisely the conditions which allow it to happen. As the poet Dylan Thomas expresses it in the beautiful lines with which this chapter began, "Time held me green and dying, though I sang in my chains like the sea." It is the reality of the chains that creates the beauty of the song.

Mediator as Bridge

From a God's-eye view of creation, the real operational challenge is not sin and evil; it is posed by the vastly unequal energetic frequencies between the realms. How can the sun touch a snowflake? How can the divine radiance meet and interpenetrate created life without incinerating it? This is the ultimate metaphysical koan—to which Christianity proposes as its solution the mystery of the incarnation.

This realization, in turn, opens up a whole new line of insight into John's statement, "For God so loved the world that he gave his only Son." The Son, in this wider metaphysical context, is no longer the one who bails us out or who rescues us from our fallen state but the one who becomes our bridge between the realms. Recognizing the enormous difficulty of our mission, Jesus comes to accompany us on it, advocating for our human finitude in a way that respects its integrity but doesn't allow us to get trapped in it. As in the traditional theological understanding (but with a very different flavor), he becomes our mediator. Standing at the confluence of two vastly different orders of being, he offers his own life as the sanctuary between them.

"Become All Flame"

As we have seen already, these great metaphysical paradoxes lend themselves more easily to poetry and metaphor than to the theological scalpel. One of the classic images Christian mystics have used to portray this cosmic mediation is actually very ancient, from the Old Testament. In the book of Exodus (3:1–6) the story is told of how Moses, while tending his father-in-law's flock of sheep in the Midianite wilderness, suddenly comes upon a bush fully engulfed in flame and yet miraculously intact. The miracle is quickly revealed as an angel of God speaking through the flame. But for the Christian desert hermits later inhabiting that same wilderness, the burning bush became a symbol of Jesus himself: all flame, yet perfectly intact within his finite container. And there were those among that desert fellowship who yearned for that same incandescent ground. In one of the most famous of the desert parables:

> Abba Lot went to Abba Joseph and said to him, "Abba, as far as I can I say my little office, I fast a little, I pray and meditate, I live in peace, and as far as I can, I purify my thoughts. What else can I do?" Then the old man stood up and stretched his hands towards heaven. His fingers became like ten lamps of fire and he said to him, "If you will, you can become all flame."[9]

Would it be possible for us, too, to "become all flame"? Could our own lives become such a perfect fusion of infinite love and finite form that light would pour from our being as an actual physical radiance? I have indeed seen this light in more than a few realized masters toward the end of their earthly journeys; it is the fully revealed mystery of human life lived as a conscious sacrament. How we get there is the secret Jesus will unfold for us through the course of his own consciously sacramental life. But our first step in joining him on this journey is to recognize that his incarnation is not about fall, guilt, or blame, but about goodness, solidarity, and our own intimate participation in the mystery of love at the heart of all creation.

9

The Passion

True love demands sacrifice, because true love is a transforming force and is really the birth-pangs of union on a higher plane.

—THE RECAPITULATION OF THE LORD'S PRAYER[1]

THE PASSION IS really the mystery of all mysteries, the heart of the Christian faith experience. By the word "passion" here we mean the events which end Jesus's earthly life: his betrayal, trial, execution on a cross, and death. Of course, for Christian believers the passion is immediately followed by the resurrection, Jesus's mysterious return to fleshly life, and later by his ascension into heaven and his disappearance from the earthly realm. These six events together comprise the full gamut of the Christian Paschal Mystery.

In the earliest centuries of Christianity, the passion and resurrection were commemorated as a single unbroken event in a ceremony that began at sunset on the eve of Easter and ended at sunrise the next morning. It was viewed as a Christian Passover. In fact, the word "paschal," which you'll sometimes hear in terms like "paschal victim" or "the paschal lamb" or "paschal candle" (or "Pâques," the French word for Easter), comes from the Hebrew *pasch,* which means "pass over." It's the same word the Jewish tradition uses to speak of its own most sacred religious festival commemorating the miraculous night when Yahweh "passed over" the houses of the Israelites but struck down the Egyptians' firstborn.[2] *Pasch* connotes the passage from death to life, and that is exactly what the earliest Christians celebrated in a single continuous ceremony.

During the fourth century the Jerusalem Christians adopted the practice of commemorating this passage "on location" as a sacred three-act drama, and over time this tradition evolved into the present Christian Holy Week. In three very intense days, Christians re-live blow-by-blow those final events of Jesus's life. Maundy Thursday depicts his last supper with the disciples and his agony in the Garden of Gethsemane as he awaits his betrayal and arrest. Good Friday presents his crucifixion, death, and burial. Holy Saturday is typically observed in silence, symbolizing the stillness of his entombment. Then Easter Sunday bursts forth in joy with the proclamation of his resurrection.

The passion has always had strong emotional charge, for obvious reasons. The spectacle of an innocent and good man destroyed by the powers of this world is an archetypal human experience. It elicits our deepest feelings of remorse and empathy (and if we're honest, our own deepest shadows as well). It has long been a popular subject of devotion in the West. It's commemorated in all the artistic genres: in the great oil canvases of Renaissance masters, in the sculpture and stained glass of the medieval cathedrals, in the English mystery plays and the German passion plays, and in music, particularly that of Bach, who gave the world his sublime St. John and St. Matthew passion oratorios. The passion is also quite manipulable. It's been used to stir anger and scapegoating. It's been used to fuel anti-Semitism, to induce personal guilt—"Christ died for your sins"—and to arouse devotion in a sentimental and even fanatical way.[3]

From a wisdom point of view, what we can we say about the passion? So much bad, manipulative, guilt-inducing theology has been based on it that it's fair to wonder whether there is any hope of starting afresh. I believe wisdom does open up that possibility. The key lies in that idea, introduced in the last chapter, of reading Jesus's life as a sacrament: a sacred mystery whose real purpose is not to arouse empathy but to *create empowerment*. In other words, Jesus is not particularly interested in increasing either your guilt or your devotion, but rather, in deepening your personal capacity to make the passage into unitive life. If you're willing to work with that wager, the passion begins to make sense in a whole new way.

I've long been struck by the question of why it should be that in Jesus's relatively short human life certain events and experiences seemed to come to him while others did not. He certainly lived in a very intense way the ordeals of betrayal, abandonment, homelessness, and death. Did it have to be like that? If he were indeed here on a divine mission, it would seem that he could have been given an easier career path: chief priest, political leader, the Messiah that people expected him to be. From any of these launching pads he would have been well positioned to "put his teachings out there" and impact the consciousness of his times in really a significant way. But none of these opportunities materialized. Why not? *Because the path he* did *walk is precisely the one that would most fully unleash the transformative power of his teaching.* It both modeled and consecrated the eye of the needle that each one of us must personally pass through in order to accomplish the "one thing necessary" here, according to his teaching: to die to self. I am not talking about literal crucifixion, of course, but I *am* talking about the literal laying down of our "life," at least as we usually recognize it. Our only truly essential human task here, Jesus teaches, is to grow beyond the survival instincts of the animal brain and egoic operating system into the kenotic joy and generosity of full human personhood. His mission was to show us how to do this. It was a mission he freely accepted. And the energy of his freedom is what ultimately raises the passion above all the emotional trappings and reveals it as a sacred path of liberation.

Moving beyond Anger and Guilt

As we get used to this new angle of vision, we probably need to begin with some deconditioning, since so many of us have grown up in that guilt-inducing theology of sacrifice and atonement. What is the meaning of the passion? First of all, God wasn't angry. Again: *God wasn't angry!* Particularly in fundamentalist theology, you'll often hear it said that God got so fed up with the sins and transgressions of Israel that he demanded a human sacrifice in atonement. But of course, this interpretation would turn God into a monster. How can Jesus, who is love, radiate and reflect a God who is primarily a monster? And how can Christians theoretically progressing on a path of love consent to live under such a reign of terror? No, we need to bury once and for all those fear-and-punishment scenarios that got programmed into so many of us during our childhood. There is no monster out there; only love waiting to set us free.

But what about "Jesus died for your sins"? Well, that foundational Christian statement is in fact completely and wholly true. But not *individually,* in the way you're most likely to hear it—Jesus died because you were bad, Jesus died because you are an alcoholic, or you beat your spouse, or cheated on your income tax. The statement doesn't work on that level. Rather, Jesus died *for*—meaning "because of" and "on behalf of"—the human condition in its collectivity. He died because of the irreducible reality—that "Planck's Constant" (to borrow a metaphor from contemporary quantum physics)—of constriction and density that comes as part and parcel of this human realm and is the necessary precondition for the full revelation of divine love (this is the challenging material we worked our way through in the last chapter). To say that he died *on behalf of us* means that he gave his life to help pull us through these difficult conditions; he implanted himself deeply at ground zero, at the root of the root of all density, in order to insulate us from its sting and empower us to live within our human flesh as he himself had lived.

Several years ago a composer friend of mine in Aspen, Colorado, offered me an unusual assignment. He was planning a new version of the passion for orchestra, chorus, and soloists, but before composing the music he wanted a new libretto, a new text to work with. Rather than simply using one of the existing gospel narratives as Bach and nearly everyone else has done, he wanted a text that would shed light on the overall meaning of the passion and eliminate those undertones of accusation and vindictiveness which so often in the past have been used to fuel religious intolerance. I leaped to the assignment; the subject had been deeply in my heart anyway. When I first sat down with my Bible and a blank legal pad, I had no idea what the process of creating this libretto would be like. What a wild ride it turned out to be! The passages I needed literally flooded into me in about five days of very intense downloading. Sometimes I would find myself being literally awakened in the middle of the night by a distinct presence, just short of an audible voice, saying, "Go to this verse" or "Use this passage next." More than any other time in my life, I felt that there was a higher hand upon me.

When I cast about for a new starting place for this passion, it turned out I did not have very far to go. It was right there under my nose in John 13–17, a profound and lovely section known as the "Farewell Discourses." With his betrayal and arrest imminent, Jesus gathers his disciples one last time to share his final instructions. What flows forth from this moment is an extraordinary series of teachings whose entire message is of love brought to its glorious fruition. These discourses contain, first and foremost, some of Jesus's most beautiful descriptions of indwelling love—for example, "I am the vine; you are the branches" (John 15:5); "As the Father has loved me, I have loved you; abide in my love" (John 15:10); "I give you a new commandment, that you love one another. Just as I have loved you, you also should love one another" (John 13:34); "[Father], the glory that you have given me, I have given them so that they may be one as we are one, I in them and you in me" (John 17:22–23). In these and similar passages we experience the intertwining mysteries of kenosis and perichoresis in their most pellucid loveliness. Even with death waiting in the wings, Jesus will allow no separation between God and humans, no separation between humans and humans, because the sap flowing through everything is love itself. In image after image he tries to impart to the disciples his assurance that they can never be cut off from that love, because their very beings are rooted in it.

Second, he tries to reassure them that this sacrifice they are about to witness, although it will be brutal, has been foreseen and is necessary. Again, the images are visually striking. In John 16:20–22, for example, he uses the analogy of childbirth to help calm their fears:

> Very truly, I tell you, you will weep and mourn, but the world will rejoice; you will have pain, but your pain will turn into joy. When a woman is in labor, she has pain, because her hour has come. But when her child is born, she no longer remembers the anguish because of the joy of having brought a human being into the world. So you have pain now, but I will see you again, and your hearts will rejoice, and no one will take your joy from you.

What a beautiful image! In a real way the disciples are about to become the midwives for such a birth as the world had never seen before: the revelation of the Kingdom of Heaven in its fullness and the inauguration of a whole new level of intimacy between the human and the divine. Just as in human childbirth, the process itself will be painful. But he assures them that the outcome will be more than they could ever possibly have imagined.

Finally, he teaches them that the approaching ordeal is absolutely essential for their own emergence; without it, they will not yet be ready to take their place in the new spiritual order about to be revealed. He reminds them, "I still have many things to say to you, but you cannot bear them now" (John 16:12). Something in their being still needs to be cured and tempered, and the sacrifice about to be consummated will achieve that alchemy. (Remember that the word "sacrifice," in its Latin roots *sacra*

facere, means "to make holy," not "to destroy.") And he promises categorically that he will not abandon them: "I will not leave
you orphaned" (John 14:18); "the Holy Spirit, whom the Father
will send in my name, will teach you everything" (John 14:26);
"In a little while the world will no longer see me, but you will
see me; because I live, you also will live" (John 14:19). At the
moment they are not quite ready, but they will become ready:
"Where I am going, you cannot follow me now" (John 13:36),
but "I will come again and will take you to myself, so that where
I am, there you may be also" (John 14:3). And in the very next
line he assures them, perhaps cryptically at this point, "You *do*
know the way to where I am going." While their outer beings
are not yet fully prepared, the inner knowingness of their hearts
is already engaged and tracking well. With this assurance he
sends them forth.

Apart from the ritual footwashing and invocation of the
New Commandment (John 13:34) during the Maundy Thursday service,[4] the Farewell Discourses do not figure prominently
in the Christian commemoration of Holy Week, at least in the
West.[5] But several years ago I had the privilege to participate in a
remarkable exception to this rule, which created one of the most
powerful Holy Week liturgies I have ever experienced. Traveling in California that spring, I had put in for Maundy Thursday at the small Trappist monastery near Vina. We were near-
ing the end of the elaborate two-hour service. The footwashing
ceremony had been enacted, Communion had been shared, the
ritual stripping of the altar and preparation of the reserve sacrament had been completed, and we were about to assemble for
the solemn monastic procession to the side chapel (where the
sacrament would lie in repose during the ensuing all-night vigil)
when the abbot called us back to our seats. As the last shafts of
sunset faded into dusk, he slowly read the whole of John 14,
about a five-minute recitation ending with Jesus's summons,
"Rise, let us be on our way." It was wrenching. I don't think
there was a dry eye in the whole church; it was as if Jesus himself was personally addressing each one of us from beyond time.
(I have since seen this same ritual performed at St. Benedict's

Monastery in Colorado, so hopefully the tradition is catching
on.) I was forcibly called back to my own deepest understanding that this sacred passion drama is not just something that
happened two thousand years ago. Each Holy Week presents us
with the opportunity, if we're willing to avail ourselves of it, to
re-live it in our hearts with fresh immediacy.

The Ultimate Kenosis

After that sending forth, the passion drama moves in earnest to
the Garden at Gethsemane, to which Jesus has withdrawn for an
all-night vigil of prayer. Having "talked the talk," he must now
walk the walk, confronting his own deepest fears and ambiva-
lence in order to come to a place where, with all his own being,
he can say, "Yes."

This is the real eye of the needle. How far can you take kenosis?
How far can you empty yourself? Does it stop at death? Do you
draw back when finally you're up against that threshold of your
most primitive fight-or-flight instincts, or do you go through?
Jesus anguishes over this, alone, in the garden. The disciples
who accompanied him have fallen asleep (a telling metaphor)!
Alone, he takes it on. The gospels do not diminish the fact that
the struggle is an agony. Luke depicts him as literally "sweat-
ing blood." On this of all occasions he is perhaps the most fully
identified with our human fragility and mortality. Finally, out of
his anguish, emerges his Yes, let it be: "Not my will but yours be
done" (Luke 22:42).

It is significant that his words here are identical with those
spoken by his mother Mary at the time of the annunciation:
"Here I am, the servant of the Lord; let it be with me according
to your word" (Luke 1:38). The Latin word for "let it be" is *fiat*,
and in both cases the human *fiat* is an essential ingredient (if not
the essential ingredient) enabling the mystery to unfold. This
coincidence becomes even more interesting when we add to our
list that third cosmic *fiat* in the book of Genesis: God said, "Let
it be!" and the created universe comes tumbling into existence.

We can begin to see that there is a tie-rod connecting "Let it be" understood as kenosis and "Let it be" understood as divine creativity. Once this point is grasped, Jesus's *fiat* in the Garden of Gethsemane is not merely a capitulation to divine necessity; it is his conscious participation in "speaking" into birth the New Creation. (And once we see even further that the same is true of every *fiat* we are able to consciously utter in our lives, then our own kenotic path comes alive with creativity and wonder.)

When I was working on my libretto for the passion, I really wanted to emphasize the sacramental nature of this fiat, its intrinsic link with birthing new life. And this became one of those occasions I alluded to earlier where I came bolt awake in the middle of the night with a couple of biblical verses weaving themselves together in my mind. The first was Jesus's beautiful metaphor in John 12 (just before the start of the Farewell Discourses): "Unless a grain of wheat falls into the earth and dies, it remains just a single grain; but if it dies, it bears much fruit." The second was a line from Psalm 126: "Those who go out weeping, bearing the seeds for sowing, shall come home with shouts of joy, carrying their sheaves." Suddenly these two unconnected texts became a single strand of meaning. I saw that in a painful but wondrous way, what is about to take place is a cosmic sowing of a seed from which will spring forth that impossible livable, the bush that burns but is not consumed.

IO

Crucifixion and Its Aftermath

He suffered under Pontius Pilate, was crucified, died, and was buried. He descended to the dead.

—THE APOSTLES' CREED

THE SILENCE OF Jesus's vigil and the stillness after his personal agony of conscience are short-lived. A raggle-taggle army arrives: palace guards of the Jewish high priests with Judas Iscariot leading the pack. Judas, Jesus's most zealous disciple, has betrayed his master for thirty pieces of silver. What must it have been like for Jesus? So quickly his "yes" has set in motion a drama that is now running at breakneck speed. There is a scurry, a scuffle. Some of the disciples grab for their swords. Jesus calls them off. "No more of this! Have you come out here with swords and clubs as if I were a bandit? When I was with you day after day in the temple, you did not lay hands on me. But this is your hour—when darkness reigns (Luke 22:51, 52 [NSRV]; Luke 22:53 [Christian Community Bible]).[1]

And so the grand spectacle begins, the grand drama of the

crucifixion. It divides into two parts: the trial, then the crucifixion itself. The scenario is admittedly complicated, reflecting
the tangled political scene in the Jerusalem of the day. Jesus is
brought first before his immediate supervisors, the Jewish high
priests, who clearly want him out of the way but lack the power,
in this Roman-dominated land, to put him to death themselves.
He is then passed on to Pontius Pilate, the Roman procurator
general, then to Herod Antipas, the Roman-backed Jewish king,
then back to Pilate, who waffles on his intuition that Jesus is innocent and allows the high priests to manipulate the crowd into a
mob scene demanding blood. If you feel that you're on a Cook's
Tour of human evil during this sequence of events, you're right.
And of course, this is Mel Gibson's turf *par excellence,* in his 2004
gut-wrenching film spectacle, *The Passion of the Christ:* the whip-
pings, the agony, the villains, the manipulations, the subplots.
It's easy to work this turf from the outside and get people very
fired up about affixing blame and scapegoating this or that particular constituency. Was it the Jews or was it the Romans?

This is the wrong question to ask. From the wisdom standpoint we need to stay grounded in the collective nature of what
is meant by "He died for our sins." The false self is ultimately
what crucified Jesus. It is an archetypal struggle. As each of the
various characters in this drama surfaces and resurfaces, we see
through the swirl the core traits of the false self in action: fear,
pretension, projection, self-importance, cowardice. In their collective mirror we can also catch, if we're honest, a glimpse of
our own unacknowledged shadows, our own particular pattern
of inner doubt and darkness. Like weathervanes, they point to
the place where we individually stop short and retreat into our
shells, drawing the line on kenotic love.

The Hall of Mirrors

The Pharisees are the easiest target, at least superficially. We easily recognize in them that telltale odor of sanctimony mixed with
self-importance, which universally presents itself as the shadow

side of religious piety. Supremely self-righteous, with murder in their hearts and yet wanting to appear as the good guys, they twist the truth to justify their actions and manipulate others into carrying out their dirty work. In his own teachings, Jesus had earlier castigated them as "hypocrites" and "a viper's brood" and compared them to whitewashed tombs: "which on the outside look beautiful, but inside they are full of the bones of the dead and of all kinds of filth" (Matthew 23:27).

When we look more closely, the Pharisees become a lot more subtle. Scholarship tells us that they were actually the *best*, not the worst, of the various Jewish religious factions; they were the "liberals" of their own times, valuing moderation and relevance. Their real undoing, however, was that endemic syndrome of religious consciousness: "twenty-twenty hindsight." While open to surface novelty, they took their bearings squarely from received tradition. They relied on the past to interpret the present, and when Jesus did not conform to their roadmaps, they trusted their roadmaps over their hearts.

What can they teach us about our own piety?

Pilate is a key figure in this drama, although the portrayal of him varies considerably in the spiritual traditions of the West. In some renditions, such as in the medieval mystery plays, he is depicted as an arch villain, a sociopath interested only in murder. In other renditions he comes across like a first-century Hamlet, fair-minded and philosophically keen but ultimately unable to carry out the course of action his heart knows to be true. He sells out for the sake of expediency, to restore a superficial peace and quiet and hang on to his own position and power. We know that aspect of the false self as well, don't we? We certainly bump into it in our politicians; where do we bump into it in ourselves?

Next, and perhaps most poignantly, come those two disciples who have gone down in history as the great betrayers: Judas and Peter. Judas's crime is the more serious, and of the two of them, he is the more psychologically complex. According to scriptural tradition, Judas was a Zealot[2] (which means that he belonged to

a political movement that was essentially the Zionism of its time).
Thus, his interest in Jesus was at least in part politically motivated. Judas saw in Jesus the long-awaited Messiah, the earthly king
who would return the nation of Israel to the glory of its former
days. Jesus was his hero, and like all hero-worshipers, Judas projected onto Jesus his own agenda—and his own personal power.
In the end what motivated his betrayal was most likely a broken
heart: too much love and too much disappointment.

Don't we all do this all the time to our own respective messiahs,
our gurus and teachers? We set them up on a pedestal, and when
they fail to carry our expectations, we tear them down, taking out
a pound of their flesh and a pound of our own as well. In Judas's
case, I believe the chief operative is despair at having hoped so
much, having invested so much of himself, and then experiencing
his hopes dashed. What the triggering incident may have been we
are not told,[3] but like any heartbroken lover he retaliates with a
desperate violence that ultimately turns self-destructive.

Finally there is Peter, whose dilemma is much more straight-
forward. With Peter it's always pretty much "what you see is what
you get," and what we see here is mostly plain old cowardice,
a massive failure of nerve when the crisis finally overtakes them.
Throughout the gospels he has repeatedly demonstrated his lack
of self-knowledge, culminating in that granddaddy of all howl-
ers on the eve of the crucifixion when he announces in complete
sincerity, "Lord, I am ready to give my life for you" (John 13:37).
But when push actually comes to shove, he finds himself fleeing
in total disarray; it is simply too dangerous to be associated with
this Jesus fellow any more. In a telling vignette (exactly predicted
by Jesus), as he huddles in the chilly first light of day warming
himself beside the last coals of a dying fire, three times he is asked
if he is one of Jesus's disciples; each time he answers, "I am not."
This seemingly harmless negation actually contains a subtle existential pun. Throughout this gospel Jesus has constantly identified himself with the power of "I am" in a series of sayings ("I
am the shepherd," "I am the door," "I am the vine," "I am at
your heart's door knocking," "I am in you and you in me," and
so forth) which are on one level simply a grammatical formula

but on another level the direct invocation of the name of God, Yahweh or "I AM." In so doing, Jesus has identified himself with being itself, and in denying his master, Peter simultaneously consigns himself to nonbeing: "I am not." But his genuine remorse once he realizes what he has done earns him his place in the passion narrative and in our hearts. Cowardly and confused though he may be, he is at least able to demonstrate that no mistake is beyond repair if it is honestly confessed and sincerely repented.

The Road to Calvary

If the arrest and trial invite us to look honestly at our own blind spots, the crucifixion itself is brutal demonstration of what ensues when this inner responsibility is avoided or projected outward. The road to Calvary quickly degenerates into a mob scene. Screaming, taunting, sadistic cruelty, and the thirst for blood all surge through the hearts and souls of this crowd of onlookers, who by their actions have been turned into animals. It's hard not to recall that pungent line from the Gospel of Thomas: "Cursed is the man whom the lion devours, for that man will become lion"—and if we think this is merely a metaphor, we have only to look closely at our own century. Jesus has earlier warned his disciples that "this is the hour when darkness reigns" (Luke 22:53); now we see played out in full brutality what happens when human collective darkness is cut loose from any moorings in individual conscience and simply runs its own fateful course. The gospels present different takes on the actual three hours of agony Jesus spent on the cross. The Gospel of John presents a Jesus stoically in command of himself throughout the entire ordeal, whose final words, "Consumatum est" ("It is completed"), suggest that he has not lost touch with the deeper meaning of this sacrifice. The other three gospels describe a scene of excruciating physical and spiritual anguish as Jesus is gradually torn loose from his inner bearings and ends his human life in the experience of utter forsakenness: "My God, my God, why have you abandoned me?" Personally, I favor that scenario

as more historically likely and also more consistent with the sacramental necessity that Jesus drink to the dregs the full anguish
of the human condition. If his sacrifice is to be fully effective, it
must penetrate all the way to the root of human darkness, and
there can be no deeper darkness than the experience of total
existential alienation and meaninglessness.[4]

"Jesus, Remember Me . . ."

Just before this final moment, however—and only in the Gospel of Luke (23:39–43)—an exchange occurs which for me has
become the real "last words of Jesus," symbolically anyway. As
Jesus hangs on his cross, flanked by two fellow criminals,[5] Luke
takes the opportunity to shape the moment into a powerful
final enactment of that drama of recognition we have spoken
about frequently throughout this book. The first criminal sees
nothing, and in an all-too-human display of petty tyranny he
wastes the final moments of his life adding his own taunts to
the mob scene: "Are you not the Messiah? Save yourself and
us!" But the other criminal reprimands him: "Do you not fear
God? We are punished justly, but this man has done nothing
wrong." Then he turns toward Jesus and (as I imagine it),
through parched lips as he nears the end of his own death
struggle, speaks the words, "Jesus, remember me when you
come into your kingdom."

What an extraordinary acknowledgment! It reveals his awareness that Jesus does indeed come from a higher order of reality, to which death will soon return him—a remarkable enough
insight in itself. But even more remarkably, it makes its plea for
a mutual bond of remembrance that will hold them together
once that reunion has taken place. In response, Jesus speaks
those immortal words: "Truly I tell you, this day you will be
with me in Paradise." Some translations say, even more powerfully, "Truly, this day you *are* with me in Paradise." The power
of recognition has already set the future in motion; it has begun
to make manifest in a small way the cosmic turning of the wheels

of love which will bind heaven and earth together in a nuptial union shortly to be consummated.

And speaking of nuptial union, it is important to remind ourselves that Jesus did not actually die alone. Though this fact is never mentioned in the Holy Week liturgies of the West, all four gospels make perfectly explicit that Mary Magdalene was there by the cross throughout the entire crucifixion and for the burial as well. It is entirely possible that she never left the site, or at best left it only briefly, to return in short order with her two fellow Maries and the burial ointments on Easter morning.[6] What the other disciples could not manage, she offered effortlessly: an unbroken witness to the power of love itself holding all things together. It is important to return her to that scene in our mind's eye, to allow her to be there in lone vigil beside the tomb. Like falcon and falconer, she holds the tether in the cosmic drama that is about to ensue.

The Harrowing of Hell

We arrive now at a strange interlude in the passion drama that many Christians are unaware of because it's not actually mentioned in scripture, only in tradition (including the Apostle's Creed); I became acutely aware of it through my earlier days as a medievalist when I staged several English mystery plays depicting the incident.

While the Bible itself makes no mention of what might have happened during those three days that Jesus lay in the tomb, there is a strong apocryphal tradition that between the time he died on the cross on Good Friday and the time he returned to the flesh on Easter Sunday, he made a visit to hell ("stormed its gates," in some accounts) in order to release the doomed souls there. In the earthy language of Middle English, this incident was known as the Harrowing of Hell.

The medieval interpretation of this legend was admittedly naïve. This visit solved a theological dilemma—namely, if in order to be saved you had to be a baptized Christian, what happened to all those good people who happened to live on the planet before Christ came? The medieval plays portray Jesus rounding up all those worthy Old Testament patriarchs—Moses with his stone tablets, David complete with harp, and a decidedly craggy Abraham—presumably in order to bring them into the Christian fold.

But setting that medieval naïveté aside, I believe the real meaning of this archetypal legend is entirely serious and deserves our full attention. In a real sense Jesus did indeed visit hell (we will see shortly what this means), and in confronting the powers and principalities there, he changed the footing on which our present world exists.

Christian theological tradition insists that it was the *death* of Christ that was the sacramental act, not his resurrection. This surprises many Christians, because it seems that resurrection is the much more obvious place where he exercised his triumph over the powers and principalities. But mystical wisdom has always intuited that the great sacramental *fiat* was actually accomplished much more quietly and inwardly in those innermost regions of the earth, as the direct outcome of his passage through death.[7]

How could this be? Let's explore further, continuing along the same line of inquiry we began in chapter 8.

I spoke in that chapter about the jagged, binary nature of this realm of existence, a reality attested to by all the great spiritual traditions. But in contrast to prevailing opinion, I tried to suggest that this state arrived through no human fault or error but as the precise conditions required to make possible a particular kind of divine self-disclosure. Only at this particular density, within these sharp edges and term limits (the ultimate one, of course, being death), do the conditions become perfect for the expression of the most tender and vulnerable aspects of divine love. Built right into the deep structure of this realm, then, is a "Planck's Constant" of darkness and density. It belongs to the warp and weft of creation itself, and to dissolve it is to cancel the very conditions through which this realm makes its uniquely important contribution to the divine fullness.

I remember first coming across this idea decades ago while I was gulping down Annie Dillard's wonderful first book, *Pilgrim at Tinker Creek*, in 1974. At the end of her powerful and disturbing chapter on "Fecundity," she wrote a paragraph that has stayed vividly with me all these years:

> That something is everywhere and always amiss is part of the very stuff of creation. It is as though each clay form had baked into it, fired into it, a blue streak of nonbeing, a shaded emptiness like a bubble that not only shapes its very structure but that also causes it to list and ultimately explode. We could have planned things more mercifully, perhaps, but our plan would never get off the drawing board until we agreed to the very compromising terms that are the only ones that being offers.
>
> The world has signed a pact with the devil; it had to. It is a covenant to which every thing, even every hydrogen atom, is bound. The terms are clear: if you want to live, you have to die . . . The world came into being with the signing of that contract.[8]

Dillard was the one who first got me to thinking in this cosmological—or *ontological,* to use the technically correct term—perspective. It had not previously occurred to me that that this irreducible brokenness might in fact be part of the givens of this realm itself. It was simply not one of the options that my classical theological training would have led me to consider. In our usual take on the Christian mystery, with the emphasis so much on personal sin, we lose sight of the fact that death and finitude really are collective, the backdrop against which everything else unfolds. Without denying our individual responsibility here, I would merely say that the boundary conditions are deeper than our individual existence. This is something the wisdom tradition has always known and insisted upon.

It seems, however, that this recognition can quickly land us in a double bind. As I mentioned earlier, virtually all the world's great spiritual traditions come with their own variation on the theme "here is not home." For the sincere mystical seeker, whose consciousness may harbor either a trace memory or a blazing inner archetype of a lighter and more fluid sphere of existence, all this brokenness seems frustrating and unnatural, and the innate tendency is to blame the problem on dualism and then collapse the tension of opposites in favor of the light. God becomes exclusively identified with goodness, light, radiance, immateriality—as the author of the First Epistle of John puts it, "God is light, and in him there is no darkness at all" (1 John 1:5)—and we have our roadmap and marching orders. The goal is to move toward the light as quickly as possible.

If only it were so! Certainly the intent of this statement is pure and true. We *wish* God could be only light. We wish this world could be only light. We wish that darkness and evil and cruelty would vanish, and we keep trying to work our way back up the great chain of being by rejecting the darkness and cleaving to the light. But darkness goes right on being dark, and the moral compass we use to navigate in some ways only makes the situation worse. For if God is light and only light, does that mean there are human states so dark and so dismal, so desolate and crazy, that they are literally "Godforsaken": outside of God altogether, completely beyond anything that the Divine can know or touch? Would that be hell? Would hell be those most alienated and broken states of consciousness, a place so fearsome that a God who is "only light and in whom there is no darkness at all" cannot enter?

A huge personal breakthrough in my own understanding of what this Harrowing of Hell mythology really is all about occurred quite unexpectedly in the midst of a discussion I had with a student a few years ago. A tenderhearted soul, she had seen the movie *Cold Mountain* the night before and had been severely disturbed by the human atrocities portrayed there. After lying awake all that night, she arrived at class in a very distressed state and asked, "How could this darkness exist? How can we remove this darkness from the planet?"

"Don't you see," I heard myself saying in response, "that by judging it you only make it worse? By trying to stop the black—to make it all white, all good; by saying that this we can accept and this we must reject, you keep empowering that cycle of polarization that creates the problem in the first place." And I think this has always been the fatal trap in the "God is light" roadmap, the orientation that cleaves to the light by trying to deny or reject the shadow. It only winds up empowering the shadow and deepening it. The resolution doesn't lie in collapsing the tension of opposites by canceling one of them out. Something has to go deeper, something that can hold them both.

Love Is Greater Than God?

One of the greatest medieval mystics, Jacob Boehme, made the challenging assertion: "God cannot enter hell, but love can enter hell and there redeem it."[9] For many years I had puzzled over the meaning of this statement. But in the very next instant of my exchange with this student, I suddenly understood what Boehme meant and what Jesus was actually up to during that pivotal moment in the passion drama. He was *just sitting there*— surrounded by the darkest, deepest, most alienated, most constricted states of pained consciousness; sitting, if we can imagine it, among all those mirroring faces of the collective false self that we encountered earlier in the crucifixion narrative: the anguish of Judas, the indecision of Pilate, the cowardice of Peter, the sanctimony of the Pharisees; sitting there in the midst of all this blackness, not judging, not fixing, just letting it be in love. And in so doing, he was allowing love to go deeper, pressing all the way to the innermost ground out of which the opposites arise and holding *that* to the light. A quiet, harmonizing love was infiltrating even the deepest places of darkness and blackness, in a way that didn't override them or cancel them, but gently reconnected them to the whole.

A beautiful poem came across my desk a few years ago, written by an anonymous English nun, which precisely captures the flavor of this deeply sacramental moment. Picturing Jesus in the last moments of his human life, she writes:

In stillness nailed.
To hold all time, all change, all circumstance in and
to Love's embrace.[10]

This single vivid image sums up the whole meaning of Jesus's
passage through the realms of hell: to hold all the boundary conditions of this realm (time, change, and circumstance) "in and
to love's embrace" and in such a way release them from the grip
of duality. You can see why Boehme and some of the other most
illumined Christian mystics have considered it a cosmic turning
point: not because a single human being personally triumphed
over the conditions of this world (an attainment attested to in
nearly all the great religious traditions), but because he did it in
such a way that did not judge or condemn these conditions but,
rather, allowed them to be as they were. In that ultimate "letting be," he transformed them into sacred vessels of divine love.
This is the mystical meaning of the great Pauline statement (in
Colossians 1:17): "In him all things hold together."

The Sun Touching a Snowflake

Does evil exist as an objective force? This has been a core question of religious seekers in all ages, and I hardly propose to
resolve it with my few final comments here. My own take on the
subject is that evil is very much a function of duality. When I say
this, I am not implying that evil is only in our minds. Duality is
an objective sphere. To that extent, evil is also an objective force
and larger than individual human subjectivity and human conscience. In those deeply hidden hours of Holy Saturday we find
Jesus going to the root of that duality, embracing it, sheathing it
in a greater love that will hold it firmly in place under the dominion of that love, and in obedience to that love, if we simply allow
the kenotic path to take its course. With that guarantee in place,
we can follow where he has gone.

This is the moment when the sun finally touches the snowflake.

II

The Great Easter Fast

WE PASS FROM Holy Saturday to Easter Sunday, from suspended waiting to a wondrous outburst of joy. From earliest times right down to our own Christians have celebrated Easter and the fifty days immediately following it as a season of great thanksgiving and triumph. The paschal sacrifice has been consummated, and love has emerged victorious. Now comes the great paschal feast when, according to an old orthodox hymn, "Christ is risen from the dead, trampling down death by death, and upon those in the tomb, bestowing life."

This season of Eastertide ("the great fifty days," as they're known in liturgical tradition) actually divides into two parts. For the first forty days Jesus is back on the planet among his friends and disciples, offering his final teaching and transmissions by way of a series of miraculous visitations known collectively as the resurrection appearances. Next comes the ascension, commemorated in the church calendar as the Thursday forty days after Easter. On this day Jesus is remembered as having ascended bodily into the skies in a dramatic final departure, recorded in the first chapter of the book of Acts. Ten days of hushed, expectant

waiting follow. Then comes the promised fiery descent of the
Holy Spirit, which Christians celebrate as Pentecost, the birthday of the church.[1]

And celebration is in order, is it not? The agonies of the passion and crucifixion are over, and the six long weeks of Lenten
fasting are behind us. Surely that's a typo in the title of this chapter. Don't I mean the great Easter *feast*?

No, "fast" is what I mean. And perhaps I am being a bit cur-
mudgeonly when I suggest that this of all Christian seasons mer-
its being kept as a fast, the Great Easter Fast. But I stick by my
guns on this point. If we really understood what is at stake in this
season—and what is spiritually possible during these exquisitely
turbo-charged days—fasting would be a small enough price to
pay. The window of opportunity is fairly narrow, but the opportunity itself is boundless.

Let me back up a bit and explain about fasting. A fast is not
about penitence and beating up on yourself. That's a very medieval attitude that totally distorts the meaning of fasting. A fast is
really training—exactly like athletic training—so that our whole
embodied being can be tuned up to support a spiritual aim we
wish to achieve. In the case of Eastertide, what's at stake—the aim
we are striving for—is our physical capacity to be available to truth
at a subtle and much more intense level. Remember how Jesus,
immediately after his baptism in the River Jordan, went into the
desert for forty days of fasting? This was not a time of penitence
and renunciation. He was actually "leaning out" his nourishment
at the physical level so that his heart would be able to listen more
deeply and his subtle energetic body might feast directly on the
flesh and blood of the divine Word stirring to life within him.[2] He
was fine-tuning his instrument so that he would be able to catch
the more subtle drift of what was awaiting him up ahead.

I believe firmly that during these great fifty days of Easter, that
same invitation is extended to each one of us: to catch the drift
of what Jesus is really inviting us to and to deepen our capacity
to receive the intense spiritual energy available to us during this
sacred season as a catapult to our own transformation—rather
than merely sloughing it off in partying and business as usual.

Jesus is headed somewhere amazing during these fifty days, and we can follow right along if we can keep up.

Now You See Him, Now You Don't

Let's look more carefully at this season of Eastertide. In the forty days immediately following Easter, as described in three of the four gospels,[3] Jesus presents himself in physical form again, walks among his disciples and friends, and reconnects with the people he has loved. Depending on how you count them and whether you take it that the gospels are describing the same event in different versions or talking about different events, there seem to be basically four of these resurrection appearances. The first is to Mary Magdalene at the tomb early on Easter Sunday (described in all four gospels). The second is in Jerusalem later that same day, when he calms the disciples as they huddle in their upper room hideaway and immediately afterward reveals himself in a graphic and powerful way to Thomas (described in John 20:19). The third is to a pair of disciples on the road to Emmaus (Luke 24:13). The fourth is once again to his disciples, but this time back in Galilee by the Lake of Tiberias (John 21). In this final appearance he shares a meal with them, helps them catch a huge load of fish, and then gives them their final instructions and commissioning. He sends them forth no longer as disciples, students, but as apostles of this new and deeper kenotic path now fully revealed.[4]

As we look at these resurrection appearances, we can see at once that there's something a bit strange about them. Jesus is back, and he is indisputably in the flesh, but it's not exactly the same flesh he left the world in. Nor does he show any indication of planning to remain here for any length of time. He doesn't reappear in Jerusalem, unpack his bags, so to speak, and start rounding up backers to found the Jesus Christ Institute of Spiritual Transformation. He could have done that, certainly (or at least its first century counterpart), and no one would have been able to stop him. But we sense from the start that he is here only temporarily and that these appearances are fleeting and ephemeral, straining toward a higher purpose that has to be accomplished in a short amount of time. Certainly his physical body is completely real and three-dimensional, as his encounter with Thomas demonstrates in a dramatic way. When Thomas insists, "Unless I see the mark of his nails in his hands, and put my finger in the mark of the nails and my hand in his side, I will not believe" (John 20:25), Jesus invites him to do just that. And in Luke's delightful retelling of this same incident, Jesus says to his friends, "I'm hungry; do you have anything to eat?" They give him a piece of boiled fish, and he eats it before their eyes.

He is no ghost, that's for sure. And yet there is something distinctly ghostlike about his movements. He apparently walks through walls, as he did when he suddenly appeared before the disciples in the upper room that evening, and he seems capable of appearing and disappearing on the spot and of presenting himself virtually simultaneously to disciples in different geographical locations. These "now you see me, now you don't" aspects are all quite pronounced in his visit with the two disciples on the road to Emmaus. He appears out of nowhere on the road, walks alongside them for a while, breaks bread with them at dinner, and then mysteriously vanishes. Evidently his body is not under exactly the same law of gravity as our own bodies. Tradition speaks (somewhat cautiously) of his "resurrection body." It's a physical body, certainly, but of a much more subtle density: a body that's appropriate to a different realm of being, a different mansion in the Father's house.

What Part of "Yes" Don't You Understand?

Another mysterious leitmotif running through all these encounters is that Jesus is not recognized at first. Mary Magdalene mistakes him for the gardener. The disciples in Jerusalem mistake him for a ghost. The disciples on the road to Emmaus recognize him, but only in retrospect, after he has vanished. And the disciples by the Sea of Tiberias are able to identify him (by his telltale signature of abundance) only after he has miraculously heaped their fishing nets full of fish. Some writers suggest that the reason he is not recognized is that the resurrection body is ageless.[5] He would not have looked like the same Jesus who only days earlier had been tortured and executed; an archetypal, ageless Jesus would now be shining through the human form. This may be true, but to my mind, the chief operative is the point I raised in the very first chapter. The wisdom walk with Jesus is at every step of the way a recognition drama. At each new level of subtlety something in us must be able to see, to find our way to who he now is. So in these instances where there is difficulty recognizing him, Jesus is in fact holding the mirror before his friends to show them what stands in their way, what they will have to look at and work through in themselves in order to be able to see him through the light of their own hearts. Indeed, this seems actually to be the main purpose of sojourn among them. He has to take them through this drama of recognition yet one more time so that they will know beyond a shadow of doubt how to find him from the inside, how to recognize him hereafter and in all times and places when his fleshly appearance becomes yet more subtle.

The encounter with the two disciples on the road to Emmaus is a textbook study of spiritual recognition. What keeps these two good souls from recognizing their master is very clear: it's their self-pity and nostalgia. As Jesus catches up with them on the road and asks what their sadness is all about, they respond: " . . . about Jesus of Nazareth, who was a prophet mighty in deed and word before God and all the people, and how our chief priests and leaders handed him over to death and crucified him. But we had hoped that he was the one to redeem Israel" (Luke 24:18–21). Clearly they are stuck in their story, and their stuckness is what makes them unable to see the person standing right before their faces. They are trapped in the past, filled with self-pity and doubt, and no one can recognize anything in this state. What Jesus does in this case is a delightful exercise of "skillful means": he rewrites their story for them. Verse by verse he leads

them through the pertinent Old Testament scriptures, reinter-
preting their meaning in the light of himself and leading them
to the inevitable conclusion that death can't be the end. Next
he breaks bread with them in a manner directly evocative of the
Last Supper and then vanishes. Finally they get it. "Were not
our hearts burning within us while he was talking to us?" Finally
they see—and the decisive breakthrough is not so much in what
they see as in *how* they see. They have come to understand that
their attuned hearts are the instruments of recognition and that
these same attuned hearts will bind them to their risen Lord
moment by moment and forever. They have finally located their
inner homing beacon.

It's a similar case, but even more dramatically, for Mary
Magdalene. Her lover's grief is what blinds her. She has vigiled
long and hard. She has stood by Jesus until the very last moment
of his human life, bearing witness when all others had deserted.
On the morning of the resurrection she has returned faithfully
to the tomb to bring precious spices to anoint his body. Yet her
longing for his physical flesh is what fuels her overwhelming
despair, her perception that all is lost. So deeply fixated is she
upon his body suddenly missing from the tomb that when Jesus
speaks to her, she can't compute the situation; she remains totally intent upon recovering that last outpost of his physical being.
Then, in a wonderfully symbolic and sacramental moment, he
calls her by name—"Maria"—and in a torrent of ecstasy she
finally awakens. "Rabboni, Rabboni!" she cries—"My beloved
Lord!" The scales are lifted from her eyes, and she flings herself
toward him to embrace and caress, as all lovers do. But his next
words to her are a gentle dissuasion and a profound teaching
exactly where she needs to hear it: "Do not cling to me, for
I have not yet ascended to my Father." He has indeed named
the place where she was stuck. She had been able to follow the
kenotic path a good part of the distance through her deep devotion, but she was still clinging to the physical person, to a particular love story and its tragic ending. She was still looking for
Jesus as a tangible corpse, not an intangible aliveness. Only when
her perspective shifted did he come into view.

Signs and Wonders

Throughout these various resurrection appearances there is an interesting phenomenon at work which I believe conforms to a valid spiritual principle. It might seem logical that the more spiritually advanced a person is, the more they would be able to meet Jesus in a fully enfleshed resurrection appearance—"like matching like," so to speak. But in fact things seem to work the opposite way. Jesus is present in physical density only insofar as is necessary to match the density of doubt that is blocking the view. Mary Magdalene needs only to see him in order to be reassured, and so Jesus appears to her as a vision. Thomas's doubt is deeply visceral, so he receives a fully visceral resurrection appearance. And some who are particularly advanced on the path, such as John, the beloved disciple,[6] never seem to require a private visitation at all; they already grasp the whole picture in their inner insight. Jesus is corporeally present only to the degree that people cannot yet see with the eye of the heart. As the eye of the heart opens, there is more and more freedom to release the physical traces and simply allow the naked immediacy of love to meet heart to heart.

And that, of course, is where this Eastertide adventure is headed. During the forty days until his ascension, Jesus is relentlessly pushing and prodding his troops toward a new level of subtlety, like a mother bird pushing her fledglings out of the nest. "You know how to do this now," he so much as tells them. "You *do* know the way. You learned the principles as my students. And what was still lacking in you before the sacrament of my passion is no longer lacking. What once tripped you up—your fear, your doubt, your craving—no longer does so. The bridge has been crossed; I myself am that bridge. In my realized eternal nature you will have intimate access to your own realized eternal nature."

He also leaves them with some practical teachings on how to keep their hearts attuned through loving service to each other and to the world. In their final encounter by the Sea of Tiberias (John 21:15), a very interesting dialogue ensues between Jesus and Peter. The dialogue is essentially untranslatable in English because our range of verbs is not wide enough. In the English version Jesus asks Peter three times, "Peter, do you love me?" Peter answers, with growing exasperation, "Yes, Lord, you know I love you." To which Jesus responds all three times, "Feed my sheep." This dialogue seems totally cryptic until we realize that in the original Greek there are two candidates for the verb "to love." One refers to a clinging, attached, erotic love. That's the verb Peter is using when he says, "Yes, Lord, I love you"—just as a lover would love a beloved, just as Mary Magdalene was attempting to cling to Jesus in that earlier episode. But the verb Jesus uses is *agape*, describing a love which is nonattached and freely self-giving. So every time Peter approaches Jesus with his emotional, grasping love Jesus turns it around on itself and makes it flow out: "Feed my sheep." He keeps gently returning Peter to the deep, mutual indwelling of kenotic love, which is the heart of the Jesus path and through which his presence among them will always make itself known.

The training completed, Jesus then rises from the physical plane, his earthly work accomplished. He knows his disciples will be able to recognize that spirit of truth when it descends on them ten days later at Pentecost. In that remarkable grand finale (described in Acts 2:1) a rushing wind and tongues of flame suddenly descend upon them, and they are filled with the spirit and able to proclaim the gospel in all the languages known to the civilization of their times. Symbolically, at least, the spirit of truth has been planted in the hearts of all human beings.

Did It Really Happen?

What do we make of these final chapters in the great resurrection drama? There are many skeptics who say that resurrection is a myth, that Jesus never rose. I myself believe that he did, and I stand my ground with Christian tradition when I affirm that his resurrection does indeed make a profound difference to how we live our lives here and now. I am not saying this out of blind adherence to any creedal statements, but out of my own inner work. In this work I have been helped immeasurably by spiritual teachers from other traditions who maintain that taking up one's body after death is by no means *that* unusual a spiritual feat. When a certain level of spiritual luminosity has been attained (which Jesus certainly manifested) it's not in fact all that difficult to regenerate physical form. And in fact, this is exactly what Jesus himself seems to be talking about in logion 22 in the Gospel of Thomas:

> When you are able to fashion
> an eye to replace an eye,
> and form a hand in place of a hand,
> or a foot for a foot,
> making one image supercede another
> —then you will enter in.

Once your temporal being (the "image" in the language of the Gospel of Thomas) has become profoundly fused with its causal archetype (its "icon," according to Thomas) so that there is no longer any gap or dissonance between them (in other words, according to this logion, "when you are able to make two become one"), then the temporal form can be put down or picked up again at one's conscious volition—though always for good reason, for spiritual servanthood and not for personal glory. A whole stream of spiritual teaching testifies that not only Jesus but many others have done this, and that in and of itself it merely confirms a very advanced spiritual being, not necessarily a cosmic singularity.[7] The question of whether Jesus *uniquely* rose from the dead, or whether that makes him *uniquely* the Son of God, is probably not the right question to be asking.

The real point is this: what Jesus does so profoundly demonstrate to us in his passage from death to life is that the walls between the realms are paper thin. Along the entire ray of creation, the "mansions" are interpenetrating and mutually permeable by love. The death of our physical form is not the death of our individual personhood. Our personhood remains alive and well, "hidden with Christ in God" (to use Paul's beautiful phrase in Colossians 3:3) and here and now we can draw strength from it (and him) to live our temporal lives with all the fullness of eternity. If we can simply keep our hearts wrapped around this core point, the rest of the Christian path begins to fall into place.

The Mystical Body of Christ

Yes, his physical form no longer walks the planet. But if we take him at his word, that poses no disruption to intimacy if we merely learn to recognize him at that other level, just as he has modeled for his disciples during those first forty days of Eastertide.

Nor has that intimacy subsided in two thousand years—at least according to the testimony of a long lineage of Christian mystics, who in a single voice proclaim that our whole universe is profoundly permeated with the presence of Christ. He surrounds, fills, holds together from top to bottom this human sphere in which we dwell. The entire cosmos has become his body, so to speak, and the blood flowing through it is his love. These are not statements that can be scientifically corroborated, but they do seem to ring true to the mystically attuned heart. And as we saw in the last chapter, these same mystical visionaries have tended to claim that this "pan-cosmic" saturation of his being into the deepest marrow of this created world was the cosmic cornerstone turned in his passage through death.[8] Without in any way denying or overriding the conditions of this earth plane, he has interpenetrated them fully, infused them with his own interior spaciousness, and invited us all into this invisible but profoundly coherent energetic field so that we may live as one body—the "Mystical Body of Christ," as it's known in Christian tradition—manifesting the Kingdom of Heaven here and now. Jesus in his ascended state is not farther removed from human beings but more intimately connected with them. He is the integral ground, the ambient wholeness within which our contingent human lives are always rooted and from which we are always receiving the help we need to keep moving ahead on the difficult walk we have to walk here. When the eye of our own heart is open and aligned within this field of perception, we recognize whom we're walking with.[9]

One person whose heart's eye was certainly wide open was the eleventh-century Greek Orthodox spiritual master Simeon the New Theologian. In a particularly fresh and intimate way, his poem "Christ's Body" speaks of the wondrous intertwining of Christ's being with our own and of the healing love that pours forth from this embrace:

> We awaken in Christ's body
> as Christ awakens our bodies,
> and my poor hand is Christ. He enters
> my foot and is infinitely me.
>
> I move my hand, and wonderfully
> my hand becomes Christ, becomes all of Him
> (for God is indivisibly
> whole, seamless in his Godhood).
>
> I move my foot, and at once
> He appears in a flash of lightning.
> Do my words seem blasphemous? —Then
> open your heart to Him
>
> And let yourself receive the one
> who is opening to you so deeply.
> For if we genuinely love Him,
> We wake up inside Christ's body
>
> Where all our body, all over,
> every most hidden part of it,
> is realized in joy as Him.
> And he makes us utterly real.
>
> And everything that is hurt, everything
> that seemed to us dark, harsh, shameful,

maimed, ugly, irreparably
damaged, is in him transformed

and recognized as whole, lovely,
radiant in his light.
We awaken as the Beloved
in every last part of our body.[10]

Try it. Move your hand, your foot. In a flash of lightning does
it become Christ? All of him? Probably not, in all honesty. Not
for me either, most of the time. For most of us, most of the time,
this notion of the mystical body of Christ surrounding and sustaining all remains an abstract concept. It's like staring into one
of those maddening dot matrix pictures, trying to see the flower
hidden in the dots. Most of the time the flower remains frustratingly elusive. We don't often see that body of Christ hidden in
the dots of our everyday, ordinary lives. But every so often, if
you let it, it will come to meet you; and with the patient opening
of the eye of your heart it can become more and more an abiding state of your own being.

Encountering the Wisdom Jesus

Which brings us to the question of praxis. As we move now into
the final part of this book, I'd like to leave you with a wager,
and "a wager" is exactly what I mean. A wager is not something
that gets rammed down your throat; it's more that same kind of
invitation Jesus issued two thousand years ago when his disciples
said, "Master, where do you come from?" And he said, "Come
and see." The wager is this: that Jesus, the living master, is real,
alive, intimately and vibrantly enfolding you right now. He is
more present, in fact, than even your breath and your heartbeat.
But to really know this presence you need to tune in on a different wavelength: to shift from your usual binary operating system to the heart frequency where this Jesus connection broad-
casts. Wisdom Christianity is practice-driven. When you do the

practices that nurture the heart, you will sense this connection as a living bond. Your being becomes receptive to the higher meaning. When the practices that sustain this encounter begin to drop out, you revert back to your usual operating system, and the connection fades.

In other words, you are the vessel, the instrument that receives the wisdom. As you attune and fine-tune your instrument, you will know. It's not knowing something more, like a new fact or piece of esoteric information; it's knowing *deeper*, knowing with more and more of your being engaged.

In the final part of this book we will be looking at five core practices you can work with right here and now—wherever you may be and whatever your life circumstances are— to awaken or deepen this wisdom connection. But one last clarification before we begin. You may have the impression when I talk about "going deeper into your heart to discover the living Christ" that I mean a subjective emotional experience. I don't. The wisdom tradition has always taught that the subjective (what we call "subjective" anyway)[11] is really introduced by your personality, sustained by the binary operating system. When you go deeper than that, when you tunnel beneath it to the still waters, you are actually able to mirror a truth that is in a final sense objective, hence recognizable as truth to all hearts that are open at that same level. "Blessed are the pure in heart, for they shall see God." Remember that beatitude? The demand for purification is real, of course, and revelation gets abused when people simply download celestial insights into their own untamed egos. This is largely the reason that the church became afraid of wisdom in the first place and opted instead for simple, concrete creeds and practices that might not have yielded great mystical insight, but at least protected the system from rampant abuse.

But we must not throw the baby out with the bathwater. Real singleness of heart is hard to come by. It takes much patient practice and purification. But Jesus himself does promise that the spirit of truth lies within you, and it connects with reality, not just your subjective meanderings. So in the spirit of that wager, let's look at the practices.

PART THREE

Christian Wisdom Practices

12

Centering Prayer Meditation

Serene light shining in the ground of my being,
draw me to yourself.
Draw me past the snares of the senses,
out of the mazes of the mind,
Free me from symbols, from words
that I may discover the signified:
the word unspoken in the darkness
that veils the ground of my being.

—BYZANTINE HYMN

HOW DO I move beyond "the mazes of the mind" and into a deeper wisdom knowing? The answer is simple, though perhaps not easy: through meditation. Meditation is one of the most ancient and universal of all spiritual practices, and it is the cornerstone of the wisdom encounter with Christ. You may already be familiar with the benefits of meditation in terms of relieving stress or relaxing the mind or the body, but its real value in terms of wisdom is to transform the way you think. Its immediate and obvious effect is to break the tyranny of your usual mind, with its constant compulsive thinking. Its underlying and far more powerful effect is to catapult you into a direct experience of being itself, unmediated by thinking, and to give you a strong taste of what heart perception actually feels like. Meditation is the tool you use to "upgrade your operating system," to move from that "either/or" thinking of the binary mind into the more spacious heart awareness that sustains the wisdom way of knowing.

Meditation practices come in a variety of flavors, each with its own particular way of quieting the ordinary mind and taking you deeper into being. Perhaps you have a practice already, and if so, I would encourage you to stay with it. But if not, or if for some reason the practices you've tried haven't stuck, I invite you to learn the method I use: Centering Prayer. I was introduced to the practice nearly twenty years ago by Father Thomas Keating, that great patriarch of the Christian contemplative reawakening, and I can attest that it has made a decisive difference in how I live my Christianity. In this chapter I will give you an overview of Centering Prayer followed by a quick walk-through, which should be enough to get you up and running in the practice. If you want to go deeper, there are any number of books, CDs, and workshops available to help put flesh on the bones of these barebones instructions, including my own *Centering Prayer and Inner Awakening*.[1]

Among the various worldwide meditation traditions, Centering Prayer is somewhat innovative. You might think that all meditation is about achieving "still mind" or "single-pointed concentration" or "pristine awareness." In fact, most meditation practices do have these as their goals. But Centering Prayer doesn't work with the mind at all; it goes straight for the heart. It's a surrender method, pure and simple, a practice based entirely on the prompt letting go of thoughts as they arise. I often think of it as kenosis in meditation form, a way of patterning into our being that continuously repeated gesture of "let go, let go, let go" at the core of the path that Jesus himself walked.

Because of this underlying theological congruence, Centering Prayer has a particular resonance with the emotional heart of Christianity and will take you very quickly into that heart.

It's a warm practice, a little sloppier and dreamier than the classic methods of attention and awareness practices. You will lose some time in daydreaming, at least at the start, and that vibrant, tingling sense of "I am here" prized in so many meditation practices is not really a goal in Centering Prayer. But its path will lead you directly to that place where, as St. Paul described it in his letter to the Romans, "the spirit prays within you," and the spirit knows what is in your heart.

The Method at a Glance

Here are the three basic points to keep in mind as you get oriented in the practice of Centering Prayer. First, Centering Prayer works entirely with the energy of intention. Most of the classic meditation practices work with *attention* rather than directly with intention; you learn to tether your "monkey mind" by giving it something simple to do, like following your breath or repeating a mantra. Centering prayer relies only on your intention, your "naked intent direct to God," as it's called in that medieval classic *The Cloud of Unknowing*.[2] To the extent that your intention is clear and strong, your practice will be also. If your intention gets muddled and confused, so will your practice. So it's important to be as clear as you can, before you even sit down on your prayer bench or chair, about what your aim is in doing so and about whether you're really willing to give yourself to it utterly. I don't mean that you need to put this aim into words (most people can't)—only that you know from the inside what you are about and are willing to give it an honest try.

Generally speaking, you are in the right ballpark if your aim is to be deeply available to God—that is, available at the depths of your being, deeper than words, memories, emotions, sensations; deeper even than your felt sense of "I am here." You are simply asked to attend, to give yourself completely into that deeper, mysterious presence.

Notice that I did *not* propose as an aim making yourself empty or making yourself still. Don't even go there. Like trying not to think of an elephant, it pretty much assures that your Centering Prayer period will be a constant, nonstop stream of thoughts. Let go of all attachment to outcome, all notions of some ideal state that you identify as meditation. Simply stay with that quiet, gathered waiting within.

Putting Teeth in Your Intention

Intention is everything in Centering Prayer, but as we all know, "the road to hell is paved with good intentions." You can sit down on your prayer mat with every intention of being totally open to God, but not thirty seconds later your mind has gotten caught up in some elaborate scenario like dreaming ahead to that hiking trip in the mountains next weekend or reliving the fight you had with your boss just before the workday ended. So in Centering Prayer there is a need to "put teeth in our intention," and the way this is done is through a simple inner agreement which I am perfectly happy to call a "deal." The deal is this: If you catch yourself thinking, you let the thought go. Promptly, quietly, without self-recrimination, you simply release the thought and start over. This is the essence of the method of Centering Prayer. Thomas Keating illustrates the point beautifully in a story by now legendary among teachers and practitioners of Centering Prayer. At one of his earliest training workshops, a nun tried out her first twenty-minute taste of Centering Prayer and then lamented, "Oh, Father Thomas, I'm such a failure at this prayer. In twenty minutes I've had ten thousand thoughts." "How lovely," responded Thomas Keating without missing a beat. "Ten thousand opportunities to return to God!" Centering prayer is indeed a pathway of return, almost entirely so. The effectiveness of this method is not measured by your ability to maintain your mind in a steady state of clarity, openness, or stillness. It is measured by your willingness, when you find itself "caught out" by a thought,[3] to return again and again and again—ten thousand times if necessary—to that state of open receptivity.

If you've got that, you've basically got the method of Centering Prayer. But one small refinement is still in order. To help grease the skids of this "letting go" motion, allowing you to release a thought promptly and easily, Centering Prayer recommends the use of a something called a "sacred word." This is a short (one or two syllables) word or phrase that symbolizes your willingness to "do the deal." It could be a classic prayer word, like "spirit" or "Jesus" or "Come, Lord," or it could be a word or phrase suggesting a mood of inner receptivity, like "open," "return," "deep," "be here," "yes." You choose the word yourself, or you can ask the Holy Spirit to choose it for you if you're more comfortable with that language. Either way, it functions like a finger pointing at the moon of your intention. It is not a classic mantra, because you don't say it constantly, only when something in you recognizes that you've gotten tangled up in a thought. At that very moment you'll find it emerging out of your unconscious to help you let go of the thought without a lot of mental agitation.

To summarize, the three basic principles of Centering Prayer are:

1. Be clear about your basic intention.
2. "Do the deal": if you catch yourself thinking, you let the thought go.
3. Use your sacred word to help release the thought promptly (without mental or emotional reaction) and return to a state of open availability.

Your First Walk-Through

That's the basic theory of Centering Prayer; now let's see what it looks like in actual practice. First, sit down on your chair (or on your prayer bench or a cushion or mat; it doesn't matter which). Your posture should be relaxed but alert. Sit as upright as you can without making yourself tense or straining your back. Your legs should be uncrossed,[4] and your head should be balanced on your shoulders, neither drooping down nor scrunched up. Basically, it's the same as good singing posture and will help your body to do its part in this prayer, which is to support you physically while making itself largely invisible. Your eyes are closed, since this is a prayer of temporary withdrawal from the stimulation of the outer world. But common sense prevails: if you find yourself falling asleep, open your eyes and refocus for a few moments, and you'll wake right back up.

You may want to ease your way into Centering Prayer with a short prayer sentence such as "Into your hands I commend my spirit" or "Be still and know that I am God"; with a chant or psalm (see ahead, chapter 14); or by taking a couple of intentional breaths. Sometimes it helps to ask yourself directly, "Am I really willing to sit here for the next twenty minutes and 'do the deal' to the best of my ability?" However you get yourself collected is fine, but Centering Prayer itself actually begins the moment you begin to "say" your sacred word—not out loud, of course, but silently, gently, and at first steadily as you ease yourself into the deeper waters.

The next step in this process is the crucial one, and it's also the hardest to explain. The usual instructions go something like this: "When you notice you're no longer being attracted to thinking, it's okay to let the sacred word go." But of course, these instructions are self-canceling, and a lot of people have gotten snarled up on them. How can you "notice" you're not thinking without thinking? How can you "decide" to let the sacred word go without that itself being a thought?

In fact, what really goes on at this step is utterly simple and natural if you can just let it be. The word drops out on its own; you don't have to decide to drop it. Very much like falling asleep at night, you can't see the moment when it happens. The unseen moment when your sacred word quietly slips away has been pre-programmed into your unconsciousness as part and parcel of your core intention to let yourself be deeply open to God. The hard work is already taken care of by the strength of your intention. So you won't see the moment when you stop thinking. What you'll notice (if you're alert) is the moment when you *start* thinking again. Something in you "comes to" and realizes you've strayed off course; now you're tangled up in a thought. Perhaps it's just a harmless little thought, like wondering what to have for supper tonight, or perhaps you're suddenly reliving some huge emotional conundrum. Whatever the content, you simply use your sacred word to let go of the thought and return to silence. If another thought comes right on the heels of the first, and another on the heels of that, you just keep patiently letting them go.

That's the basic practice. You do it for twenty minutes. Then, when the time is up, slowly open your eyes and without any sort of rush or violence allow yourself to come back into your usual state of consciousness. Take a minute or two for this transition, then get up and move about your business.

For most people, a typical Centering Prayer period looks a bit like a sine wave: a lot of ups and downs. There are moments when the mind is restless and jumpy and thoughts come one on top of another. There are also moments of stillness, sometimes very deep stillness. You won't be able to retrieve these moments directly, of course, because as soon as you start thinking about them they're gone. But you will "remember" them through a certain quiet gathered-ness that accompanies you as you get up and move about your day. Through the cumulative energy of this gathered stillness, Centering Prayer gradually imprints itself deeply on your heart.

How do I know when the twenty minutes are over? A good question. You can set a timer, if you can find one that doesn't send you through the roof when it goes off. Some people make themselves a personalized meditation tape. After two or three minutes of their favorite quieting music, the tape runs in silence for twenty minutes, then slowly brings the music back in again to signal the end of the meditation. My own solution is even simpler: I just look at my watch.

Incidentally, there's nothing sacred about twenty minutes. Thomas Keating suggests that this is the minimum amount of time most people need to really settle into the practice and get a taste of what lies beyond the monkey mind. You can meditate for twenty-five minutes if you want, or thirty, or even a bit more.[5] The important thing is to decide in advance how long you plan to sit for, then stick with your plan. That diminishes the risk of letting the length of your meditation get tied to your subjective experience of how the process is going: "I'm having a deep, great meditation; I think I'll go longer," or "Oh, this is hard, I'm having lots of thoughts. I think I'll stop." Centering prayer is not about having great experiences; it's about doing the practice no matter what the subjective experience may be. Sometimes those prayer practices that feel the hardest are the ones where the most inner ground is actually being gained.

Praxis Makes Perfect

Any form of meditation practice needs to be patterned into your life as a regular habit; only then can it do its real work of transforming your consciousness. Father Keating recommends that the "standard dosage" for Centering Prayer should be twenty minutes twice a day, the optimal times being early morning upon awakening and sometime during the evening hours (but not immediately before bedtime; it can sometimes keep you awake at night). I heartily agree with this advice and encourage you to apply it if at all possible. But if you are one of those people whose schedule feels completely "maxed out," I would rather see you get one period of Centering Prayer up and running than postpone the whole project because you can't see your way clear to two. Pick whatever time of day offers your best chance for twenty minutes of uninterrupted silence, and do the practice then. A regular time slot is best, but if even that won't work, simply make a commitment to practice each day wherever the window of opportunity opens up. The important thing is to begin *somewhere,* not just daydream about starting when the outside world calms down (it never will). If you can simply take the first step of planting the practice somewhere in your daily schedule, the practice itself will begin to do the rest, gradually transforming your priorities from the inside out. One of my busy friends who claimed never to have time for Centering Prayer was finally able to make a commitment to the practice when he suddenly realized, "Hmm, in all my busy life I've never missed a meal." We invest huge amounts of time in our physical well being, but this other type of well being, this birthing of your deeper heart awareness, may just be the most important thing you ever do. It lays the foundation not just for this world, but for all the worlds, open and immediate to you in the resonance of your heart.

13

Lectio Divina

HOW DO I begin to read the Bible from that deeper wisdom perspective? A very good question! Many people feel intimidated diving into the scriptures by themselves, convinced that one must be a biblical scholar to have the authority to proceed. But this simply isn't so. For fifteen hundred years Christian monks—and now increasing numbers of lay people—have been using a practice called *lectio divina* (Latin for "sacred reading") to carry them deeper into their own heart-knowing. It's a simple yet profound way of praying the scripture that transcends mental processing in favor of a deeper form of spiritual ingestion. In fact, the early monks talked about "ruminating" scripture: not ruminating *on* scripture (as in pondering it), but ruminating it like a cow chewing its cud. Lectio divina is a time-tested way of "chewing scripture"—feeding on it, absorbing it deeply into one's being where, like all food, it provides nurturance and the energy for growth.

This implies, of course, that scripture is food—and that is indeed the underlying presupposition in lectio divina. The practice is based on the wager that scripture is a *living* word—not just history, not just facts and figures you can read in a book, but a source of ongoing personal guidance that can speak in your heart here and now, offering insight and uncannily timely assistance. I used the word "wager" deliberately, for as in all wisdom work, nothing is to be accepted on blind faith. But people who work with lectio divina on a regular basis report overwhelmingly that the wager holds true. If you open yourself to this practice with any degree of inner receptivity, it is amazing how often you will be led to exactly what you need to hear at the moment or exactly the kick in the pants you need to get you moving.

In lectio divina you work intensely with a short scriptural passage in four distinct steps called *lectio* (reading), *meditatio* (reflection), *oratio* (prayer), and *contemplatio* (contemplation). These steps are usually presented as sequential, although this is by no means an ironclad rule. Experienced practitioners will often experience lectio as essentially a circular process, with the steps unfolding in any order. As we begin to acquaint ourselves with the practice, however, it makes sense to keep them in the traditional sequence.

Living Water

For our first walk-through, let's work with a portion of John 4, the dialogue between Jesus and the woman at the well that we first explored all the way back in chapter 1. Collect yourself with a moment of silence or a brief prayer, then read the following passage slowly and, if possible, aloud As your eyes moves over the page, allow yourself to be drawn to a sentence, a phrase, or even a single word that somehow seems to pique your interest or curiosity. Here is the text:

> Jesus, tired out by his journey, was sitting by the well. It was about noon. A Samaritan woman came to draw water, and Jesus said to her, "Give me a drink." (His disciples had gone to the city to buy food.) The Samaritan woman said to him, "How is it that you, a Jew, ask a drink of me, a woman of Samaria?" (Jews do not share things in common with Samaritans.) Jesus answered

her, "If you knew the gift of God, and who it is that is
saying to you, 'Give me a drink,' you would have asked
him, and he would have given you living water." The
woman said to him, "Sir, you have no bucket, and the
well is deep. Where do you get that living water? Are
you greater than our ancestor Jacob, who gave us the
well, and with his sons and flocks drank from it?" Jesus
said to her, "Everyone who drinks of this water will be
thirsty again, but those who drink of the water that I
will give them will never be thirsty. The water that I will
give will become in them a spring of water gushing up
to eternal life." The woman said to him, "Sir, give me
this water, so that I may never be thirsty, or have to keep
coming here to draw water."

This slow, attentive reading is called lectio, the first step in the
process. If you wish to, pause for a moment of silence, then read
it again. While you are reading you are also actively listening.

Getting the knack of this first step is a matter of learning to
follow the movement of your own spirit as it draws you to the
specific nugget of the text that will furnish your daily bread.
Perhaps it's Jesus's striking assurance, "Those who drink of the
water I give them will never be thirsty," or those beautiful words
the woman speaks in response: "Give me this water so that I
may never be thirsty." Perhaps it's something simpler, like the
phrase "living water," or even something out of left field, like
the words, "Sir, you have no bucket." The important point is
not *what* you're struck by, but *that* you're stuck by it—that is,
your willingness to trust that as you open to the passage in this
deeply listening and receptive way, something will indeed be
calling. Stick with it; follow its lead.

Engaging the Text

The second step in lectio is known as meditatio, or "meditation,"
which in the spiritual vocabulary of the West has traditionally

meant focused mental reflection. In this stage you quietly allow your faculties—your reason, your imagination, your memory and your emotions—to begin to work with the passage. The process will be a bit different each time. Sometimes the passage you're working with might trigger an association from your own life, or it might stimulate your thinking or confuse you, or even make you angry. See if you can discover why. Or you might be struck by a certain wordplay or turn of phrase or compelling image—"a spring of water gushing up to eternal life," for example. Another very effective way of working with a text is to role play one of the characters. Imagine yourself as the woman at the well and see if you can follow her movements internally at each step in this remarkable dialogue. Or picture yourself in the role of Jesus (what better way to put on the mind of Christ?) and see where it leads you. Suppose, for example, that you hear yourself forming his words, "Give me a drink," and are suddenly struck by the notion, "Hmmm . . . even Jesus got thirsty from time to time. Did he really have human needs? Is there something he needs from us? From *me*?"

These are just a few suggestions to help you find your own way into meditation. Whatever catches your attention, stay with it and work with it. Bring all your imagination to bear upon it. But remember, this is not biblical research. Don't reach for the scholarly commentaries or concordances—not now, anyway. This practice is not about acquiring information or learning what the experts have to say; it is about allowing the text to break open and resonate in the authority of your own heart.

The third stage in the process is called oratio, which in Latin means "prayer." If feelings arise in you out of this heart-to-heart encounter with scripture, let the feelings happen. Sit with them quietly and see if they want to shape themselves into a prayer. You might discover, for example, that the words, "Give me this water, so that I may never be thirsty" exactly express your own deepest spiritual yearning. Pray them that way, then: let them become the words of your own heart. Or perhaps something in the text will move you deeply or even fill you with tears of remorse or gratitude. Say, for example, that you are pondering the notion, "Does

Jesus really need something from me?" Suddenly you are struck by the realization that there is a deep mutuality in the encounter; your gift counts. A sense of intimacy floods through your being, and you are filled with gratitude. Let the feelings flow; this is oratio at its exquisite best, the moment when, in St. Paul's words, the spirit begins to pray within you. (And remember, a prayer doesn't always have to be in words; the feelings themselves can be the prayer.)

Sometimes this moment just doesn't happen. You'll sit with a passage, and even though you've given it your very best, it still doesn't move you to prayer. Don't worry. Don't fake it; don't force yourself to have an emotional encounter with the text if the feelings simply are not there. If nothing is stirring for you in the oratio department today, just go on to the next step.

"Resting in God"

The final step in lectio divina is known as contemplatio, which in monastic tradition is traditionally described as "resting in God." The phrase itself comes from the sixth-century church father St. Gregory the Great, but the feeling it evokes harkens back to a much more ancient text, Psalm 131, which monks to this day are fond of quoting to describe the essence of contemplatio:

> O Lord, I am not proud;
> I have no haughty looks.
>
> I do not occupy myself with great matters,
> or with things that are too hard for me.
>
> But I still my soul and make it quiet,
> like a [weaned] child upon its mother's breast;
> My soul is quieted within me.[1]

A weaned child on its mother's lap is no longer hungry; filled to satisfaction, it merely rests and allows digestion to take place.

In exactly the same way, at this stage of lectio you suspend all mental and emotional activity and simply "rest" in the fullness of the feast. The digestive work goes on beneath the level of your conscious mind.

If you think this step sounds a bit like Centering Prayer, you are exactly right. When Father Thomas Keating and his monastic brethren at St. Joseph's Abbey in Massachusetts first developed the practice during the mid 1970s, they saw themselves as essentially extrapolating the silent resting of the fourth stage of lectio and reframing it as a stand-alone meditation practice. If you have the time available to you, you can certainly practice Centering Prayer within its original monastic niche, and the fruits are palpable. But as is always the case when monastic practices are exported into the very different circumstances of secular life, sustainability needs to be your bottom line. Don't bite off more than you can chew.

Speaking of which, how *much* time needs to be allotted for this practice? Classically a monk will work with lectio for one or even two hours in his or her cell, going through the steps not just once but sometimes several times, and not necessarily in any set order. While lectio, meditatio, oratio, contemplatio, is the traditional sequence, experienced practitioners tend to follow the movement of the spirit, weaving between the steps in a wonderfully fluid way. Sometimes meditatio will lead directly to contemplatio, then back to oratio as the silent depths fashion the prayer of the heart. Occasionally lectio will lead straight to oratio, then slowly release you back into meditatio—or push you straight into contemplatio. Once you get the hang of it, it's like dancing with an invisible partner. If you have half an hour a day to give to this practice, or even half an hour every other day, you'll begin to see dramatic differences in your intimacy level with scripture. Those words and images you chew on during your time of lectio will continue to percolate beneath the surface of your day, shaping what you see and do in ways you could never have imagined.

Incidentally, the passage we just worked with is at the absolute maximum end of the spectrum in terms of length. You could cut it in half, and it would still be more than ample as a lectio text. I know many monks who work with a single sentence—or even a single word—sometimes for days, until the text finally reveals its hidden treasure. Generally three or four sentences is ideal.

Where Do I Start?

Traditionally when monks speak of lectio divina, they have in mind that the book you are working with is the Bible. Other sources, no matter how worthy or enlightening, do not officially qualify as lectio texts. Of course all things change, and the traditional practice of lectio developed in an era far less culturally and interspiritually open than our own. Certainly you can take the basic practice of attentive inner listening and use it with any sacred text of the Christian tradition or any spiritual tradition. It's magical to do lectio with Rumi, with the Dhammapada (the sayings of the Buddha), with the Upanishads, or with the Gospel of Thomas. In that sense the practice is generic and transferable to any texts that deeply touch your heart. But it is important to keep in mind that if you are walking the Christian path, the Bible has a special preeminence. It has been "living water" for generation upon generation of Christian saints and seekers, the context within which the Christian conversation unfolds. To truly receive into yourself the cumulative wisdom of this tradition really asks you to give primary attention to the Bible as the mainstay of your lectio divina.

So where in the Bible do you begin? That's a very good question. Basically there are two strategies. The first, and by far the least problematic, is to work with what's known as the daily lectionary. Most of the mainstream Christian denominations (Roman Catholic, Episcopal, Lutheran, Methodist, United Church, and Presbyterian) make use of a standard set of readings for Sunday and daily devotional use. You can purchase these in inexpensive published editions or obtain them from church offices or online. For each day you will find three readings: an Old Testament passage, an epistle (which means any book in the New Testament other than the four gospels), and a gospel. Choose any one of these texts and work with it during your time of lectio, or else take the readings for the upcoming Sunday and work with them a little bit at a time throughout the week: the gospel one day, the epistle the next, the Old Testament reading the next, or whatever approach works for you.

The advantage of working with the lectionary is that it provides short, prescreened doses of texts (that is, you won't spend your time wandering in the lengthy purification codes of the book of Leviticus), thematically organized around a key Christian teaching. Working with the lectionary also gives you the reinforcement of moving in solidarity with the church, if that feels helpful to you. As you study and pray your way through these texts, you'll know that thousands of other people in the world are working on these same passages in the same way (maybe even at the same time). There is a sense of spiritual heft and interconnectedness that gives deep meaning to the traditional notion of the church as the body of Christ.

The other strategy is simply to pick a book in the Bible and begin. If you opt for this method, I would suggest that you begin with the one of the gospels, since they are the primary reservoir for direct immersion in the mind of Christ. Once you have worked your way through them, enjoying their distinctly different flavors, you will be ready for the extraordinary treasure trove of mystical insight in the writings of Paul. His best known—though exceedingly difficult—works are his epistles to the Romans and to the Corinthians; as you work with these texts, particularly if you've been raised in a fundamentalist tradition, you may need to allow the deeper silence of your contemplatio to do a little deconditioning. There is a marked difference between hearing these texts as articles of dogma and morality rammed down your throat and hearing them as windows into mystical truth. You will also discover an extraordinary treasury of wisdom in those wonderful four "lesser" epistles: Galatians, Ephesians, Philippians, and Colossians. As you work through these texts, you will discover at least a half dozen of what can only be called "sacred hymns" (the kenosis passage in Philippians 2:9–16 is one of these): passages where the brilliance of Paul's insight and the beauty of his poetry melt together into a pure soul music.

The psalms are a perennial rich ground for lectio divina, and the tradition of working with them this way actually precedes Christianity by a good thousand years. I once asked Father Theophane, the guestmaster at St. Benedict's Monastery, about the monastic tradition's great affection for the psalms. His ready answer was: "I like to think I'm praying in the same words that Christ used." It is indeed a bit mind-bending to imagine Jesus working with the psalms in much the same way as you yourself are now working, ingesting their images deep into his being and allowing them to form his basic vessel of self-understanding. To a lesser degree, the same holds true for those other beautiful wisdom texts of the Old Testament: Ecclesiastes, Proverbs, Job, and the Song of Songs. The beautiful imagery and deep contemplative wisdom of these texts were the nurturing ground in which Jesus himself came to consciousness.[2]

If you work at this process long and patiently enough, you may eventually cover the entire Bible. My hermit teacher at St. Benedict's Monastery, Brother Raphael, had in fact done this not only once, but five times: cover to cover, beginning in Genesis and ending in Revelation, two or three verses at a time. It had taken him forty years, but he loved the process; it was his daily bread.

However you choose to work with the text, remember that the goal is a long-term one: to get to know the Bible in an intimate and ongoing way, not to barrel your way through as fast as you can so as to move on to some other reading project. In the words of the Maine poet Philip Booth, "How you get there is where you'll arrive."[3]

Group Lectio

Traditionally lectio divina is done as a solitary activity, by a single monk in his or her cell. But as contemplative practice has begun to catch on among laypeople, you'll find lectio in groups becoming more and more common. This can indeed be a powerful experience and a natural complement to group Centering Prayer, although there are also challenges involved in maintaining the inner stillness and fluidity essential to the practice.

If you're thinking of forming a lectio group, the most important thing to remember is that a lectio divina group is very different from a Bible study group. You're not there to share or discuss or debate. It's much more like a group meditation that shares its space with a scriptural text. Speaking happens, but the words are always framed in silence and must never overpower it.

Here is a simple but effective format to guide the lectio process. First, designate a leader who will lead the group through the steps and keep everyone moving together. Begin with a period of silence, then have a designated person read the scriptural passage: slowly, quietly, gently. Before the actual reading, the leader should instruct each person to listen quietly for the sentence, the phrase, or even the single word that seems to call them (the process I described earlier in this chapter).

After the reading, have everyone sit in silence for another minute or two, then read the passage aloud again. After this second reading, invite each person, as they feel so moved, to speak out loud the word, the phrase, the sentence that has called to them. If someone else has already spoken "their" word, remind them that it's perfectly okay to repeat it. The effect of that repetition is actually quite magical. People will pick up very different textual threads, and the overall effect is rather like a beautiful stereophonic reading of the scripture in the act of implanting itself in each individual heart. Once that exercise has run its course, read the passage a third time and return to silence for a few more minutes. The group leader may choose to offer a closing prayer, then the group leaves in silence.

As you can see, we have only really done the first step together, and I myself prefer to leave it at that. You will find more formulaic approaches available, offering specific exercises to simulate the motions of meditatio and oratio ("Now let's have everybody name a feeling the passage touches off for them; now let's have everybody speak a prayer that arises for them out of the passage"), but I personally find this methodology artificial and constraining of the essentially fluid and personal nature of lectio. In the generous silence between the readings, people will find a space to engage in their own meditatio and oratio in whatever way seems right to them.

Living Poetry

Above all, notice that I have not asked you to discuss the passage, and observing that prohibition is really important. Traditional fellowship and sharing around the Bible, which is all well and good in its own right, pulls you back into your usual self; whereas the more contemplative approach of lectio divina, will carry you "beyond the mind" into the greater heart-knowingness we have been exploring throughout this entire book. What begins to emerge in a person from the slow, patient work in lectio divina is not only an intimate familiarity with scripture but also a distinctly poetic relationship with it—traditionally described as the awakening of the "anagogical" or unitive imagination.[4] Some of the finest preaching I have ever heard has been from monks who have sat with their text in lectio divina and explicate it almost haiku-style, in simple one-liners that are allusive, metaphorical, and hit the nail right on the head. I have carried with me for more than a decade a ten-second homily preached by a monk at St. Benedict's Monastery. The gospel that day (Matthew 4:19) described Jesus's recruitment of his first disciples from among the Galilean fishermen and concluded with the line, "at once they left their nets and followed him." The monk merely commented, "Would that we might do the same." His metaphorically attuned mind had instantly grasped that the nets those fishermen were preoccupied with are so much like the nets of our own turmoil and psychological issues that keep us stranded on the shore. Would that we could untangle ourselves! It may not have been great scholarly preaching, but it illumined the heart more than a torrent of words. This is mature lectio divina, where the poetry of scripture and the poetry of one's own life come together to form a single whole. And it can be that way for us as well. That's the wager, anyhow.

14

Chanting and Psalmody

DID YOU NOTICE during our lectio divina session what a difference there is between reading a scriptural passage silently and reading it out loud? A whole different set of faculties are engaged, and you hear the passage in an entirely new way. The difference becomes even greater when you move from saying something to *chanting* it.

Try it for yourself. Let's take as an example that shortest of all sayings in the Gospel of Thomas, logion 42:

Come into being as you pass away.

Try speaking it out loud once or twice. Then add your voice. Take a deep breath, and just begin—a single tone is fine, at whatever pitch is comfortable for you. Keep chanting for a while, at least four or five repetitions. As you cross over this simple but momentous watershed in your being, the words suddenly spring to life in a whole new way. Put a simple clapped rhythm underneath them ("one, two-and-three, four"), and you can hear how a song is beginning to grow.

Chanting is at the heart of all sacred traditions worldwide, and for very good reason: it is fundamentally a deep-immersion experience in the creative power of the universe itself. Because to make music, you must engage those three core elements out of which the earth was fashioned and through which all spiritual transformation happens.

The first element, of course, is breath. Many of the great world religions picture the earth as being created and sustained by the steady, rhythmic "breathing" of God. Virtually every tradition starts you off on a spiritual practice by bringing attention to your breath and teaching you to breathe fully and consciously. Father Theophane, whom we met in the last chapter, liked to remind his retreatants, "Every breath you take is the breath of God."

The second element is tone, or vibration, the sound you make when you add voice to that breath. Again, many of the world's sacred traditions tell us that creation came into existence through the power of vibration. Recent string theory upholds this same insight, speculating that at the root of everything—inside the quarks, the smallest known "things"—lie tiny frequency bands vibrating in strict proportion.[1] This fascinating discovery from the leading edge of quantum physics adds new power to the ancient Christian insight, "In the beginning was the Word, and the Word was with God and the Word was God" (John 1:1)—for what else is "word" but vibration combined with intentionality? Mythologically, the world was "spoken" into existence. And when we add our tone, we join this speaking.

The third element, which I just mentioned above, is intentionality. The great wisdom traditions have always claimed that the universe is not merely a random event, but the intricate unfolding of a divine intelligence and purpose—a "plan," if you will. The coherence of divine intention is what ultimately holds everything together. In much the same way, when you chant, the quality of your intention and attention is what makes the difference between boredom and beauty. As you give yourself to the words you are chanting, their spiritual power comes alive in you.

In addition to these great universals, we also know in a very personal way that singing will often bring into play a heightened range of emotion not accessible through speaking alone. The lyrics of a song—say, "Silent Night"—can look bland and harmless on a page, but when you actually sing them (particularly with others), a magical transformation occurs. Eastern masters have long been aware of the power of chanting to effect changes in the subtle energetic structure of the body; mantras are specifically assigned for this purpose. Although Westerners may sometimes feel uncomfortable with this notion and poke fun at the caricatured image of the Eastern meditator sitting with hands folded, chanting the word "om," some of our own sacred chant words, such as "amen" ("ah-men," not "ay-men"), "alleluia," and "O" (as in "O God") are unbeknownst to us producing much the same inner effect.[2]

Psalmody and the Divine Office

In the Christian tradition sacred chanting has always centered on the psalms. We saw a bit of the "why" of this in the last chapter, when I quoted Father Theophane as saying "I like to think that I'm praying in the same words that Christ used." Christianity builds on the foundation of Jewish spirituality and practice, and by the time the young Jesus was learning to sing the psalms, he was being formed in a tradition that was already more than a thousand years old. Psalmody (that is, the practice of chanting the psalms) obviously constituted a basic vessel of his self-understanding. All four gospels remember him as quoting the psalms at significant junction points in his life, most poignantly his last words on the cross: in Matthew, "My God, my God, why have you forsaken me?" (Psalm 22:1), and in Luke, "Father, into your hands I commend my spirit" (Psalm 31:5).

The earliest Christian practice around the psalms was unsystematical but intense. The desert monks simply undertook to chant the psalms one after another (from memory, of course, since both texts and the ability to read them were the exception, not the rule) as a focal point for their attention. Tradition remembers them as having chanted all 150 psalms in a day,[3] and while there is undoubtedly some exaggeration here, it is clear that psalmody was the mainstay of daily practice, interspersed with simple manual tasks such as the plaiting of rope. We know that the form of recitation was in fact chanting rather than mere speaking because of a specific comment by the fourth-century spiritual father Evagrius: "It is a great thing to pray without distraction, but to chant psalms without distraction is even better."[4] And in fact, anywhere in the Near Eastern context, chanting as the normal mode of delivery would simply be assumed. The word "psalm" in fact means "song." A spoken psalm is as much an oxymoron as a two-wheeled tricycle.

In the sixth century, St. Benedict, the great founder of monasticism in the West, simplified and codified this procedure a bit. In place of what amounted to round-the-clock chanting, he developed a system of seven specific points during the day for prayer and psalmody (and an additional longish service at night), a structure known as "the Divine Office." This term translates the Latin phrase "Opus Dei" ("the work of God"), for it was Benedict's firm conviction that the principal work of a monk was to praise God through prayer and song. The specifics of his scheme are spelled out in the Rule of St. Benedict;[5] basically, the eightfold daily office provided a means for the monks to work their way systematically through all 150 psalms in the course of a week. That system is still basically in effect in Benedictine monasteries today, although it is more common nowadays to relax the rigor a bit and cover the psalmody on a two-week cycle.[6] If you go on a monastic retreat, you will almost certainly encounter the practice; it is still the backbone of the monastic day, and the part that most retreatants remember as the high point of their retreat experience.

Of course, over the centuries, different musical styles have evolved to support this chanting. The most well known in the West is the sublime repertory of Gregorian chant, which for well over a thousand years provided the musical vehicle for the chanting of the mass and Divine Office. During the 1960s that venerable tradition underwent dramatic revision, and the current Western liturgical style favors simple psalm tones in the vernacular (although Gregorian chant seems to be slowly regaining ground). In the Eastern part of the Christian world Byzantine chant predominates, and beyond the Byzantine sphere of influence, in the Christian communities of the Near East and North Africa, the chant has a distinctly Semitic flavor to it, reminiscent of Jewish and Islamic chanting. There are also, as we shall see shortly, new styles of Christian chanting coming into popularity that move away from classic psalmody altogether in favor of the more simple, mantric chants favored by most of the great universal traditions of sacred chanting.

Chanting as Personal Practice

While most people are deeply appreciative of the sacred aura created by monastic chanting, there have to date been few resources available to help bring the practice home. I tried to address that lack in my book *Chanting the Psalms* (Shambhala, 2006). It contains a detailed explanation of the theory and background of monastic psalmody, plus practical instruction in chanting by ear and learning to read simple psalm tones (there is even a CD included with the book to help get you up to speed). I myself have been chanting the psalms morning and evening for thirty years now as part of my daily spiritual practice, and I can attest to the power of this practice to awaken the heart and support the emergence of the "unitive imagination" I referred to in the last chapter. In the brief overview here my goal is simply to offer a few basic pointers to get you started.

Chanting as a spiritual practice does not require a trained voice or the ability to read music. Basically it's as simple as opening your Bible and *beginning*—on a single note, if need be, just as we practiced with logion 42. Later, if you feel like it, you can invent your own simple melodies, known as "psalm tones" (I show you how to do this in my *Chanting the Psalms* book), or adapt ones you've heard in church or on recordings to your own personal use. With a bit of listening practice you'll find that you can pick up simple psalm tones entirely by ear. I sometimes refer to this approach as "Suzuki psalmody," after the style of music training that starts people right off playing by ear rather than tackling the task of learning to read music. In fact, that's how monks traditionally learned to chant; even the complex melodies of Gregorian chant were first learned by memorization and by ear. When you work this way, incidentally, it connects with a much deeper circuitry within your being, less tied to the mental faculties (which are engaged by sight reading) and more deeply connected to your heart. It is not by accident that this way of relating to a body of material is called "learning by heart."

Developing a System

Like the desert monks, you may be wondering, "Where do I begin?" The question of how many and which psalms you wish to fit into your day is mostly a matter of personal choice, based on how deeply and systematically you want to invest in the practice. At the "formal" end of the spectrum, you might opt for working your way regularly through the psalms in some systematic version of your own daily office. If so, there are two resources I highly recommend. The Episcopal Book of Common Prayer contains an excellent psalter (the name given to a collection of psalms), with the psalms in clean, two-line couplets (easy for Suzuki chanting), divided up into "morning prayer" and "evening prayer" at the rate of about four per office. In a month you work your way through the entire psalter. Another excellent resource is *The Work of God* by Judith Sutera.[7] It offers a barebones daily office for morning and evening (on a two-week cycle), with crisp, haiku-like translations of the psalms. You can chant this office in ten minutes flat, but with all the dignified ambience of a traditional Benedictine service.

But you do not have to tie your chanting to a formal daily office, though it's traditionally been done that way. If you can read music a bit, you will find simple, singable psalm tones for the more well-known psalms included at the back of most recent

Roman Catholic and Protestant hymnals, and also online.[8] Or you can simply buy a CD of psalmody in any style you like, from Gregorian to Byzantine to contemporary, and sing along.

Does It Have to Be the Psalms?

While the psalms definitely have pride of place in Christian contemplative tradition, it is sadly true that many contemporary seekers have become reluctant to work with them. Aside from their sheer verbosity when compared to most the world's other traditions of sacred chant, they can be rife with patriarchal language, dualistic thinking, and even gratuitous violence. Some of the most mature and conscientious Christians—even a growing number of monastic abbots and elders—are reluctantly concluding that the psalms are a luxury humankind can no longer afford.

Without prejudicing the question, I would note that the tradition is in considerable flux here, and the outcome is by no means certain. Within the context of a classic monastic practice, I believe the psalms carry the lion's share of the work of spiritual purification. Even the notorious "cursing psalms,"[9] when tethered within the Divine Office and the overall program of monastic transformation, become a mirror in which monks advancing on the path can see themselves, acknowledging (and also releasing) the shadow side in which the psalms are so steeped. One of the great desert fathers, John Cassian, attributes the psalms' powerful spiritual efficacy to the fact that they carry within them "all the feelings of which human nature is capable."[10] Simply by looking around me at my own monastic friends and role models, I can see that years of working with these pieces of poetry do not result in increased violence but more a kind of inner tempering. And the fact that the greatest of Christian saints, from Jesus to St. Francis to Thomas Merton and Thomas Keating in our own times, have all come to spiritual maturity chanting the psalms suggests that the results can't be all negative.

But as we tackle the challenge of exporting monastic contemplative practices beyond the cloister walls, allowances have to be made and adaptations developed. These processes are actively underway in contemporary Christian chanting, auguring a decidedly new shape to the ancient tradition of psalmody.

Taizé Chant

Perhaps the most powerful new development during the past thirty years has been the emergence of Taizé chant. "Taizé" (pronounced "tay-*zay*") is a tiny village in eastern France which in the late 1940s became home to an ecumenical Christian monastic community seeking to live out the gospel call to reconciliation. As the good work of this community began to be discovered during the 1970s and people started showing up on its doorsteps in ever increasing numbers, the pressure of hospitality and inclusiveness led the monks to develop a much simpler and more accessible chant form for the community's public worship.[11] In Taizé chant, a simple phrase or sentence (such as "The Lord is my light, my light and salvation; in God I trust, in God I trust") is sung over and over again, for at least five and sometimes as long as ten minutes. Many of these "refrains," as they're known, actually come from the psalms, but pruned of their violence and used instead as affirmations of God's tenderness and faithful presence. Sung to simple two-, three-, or four-part harmonies or as canons, and available in many languages, they are intended to bring groups quickly into a deep heart silence.

The chant quickly became a major draw, particularly for the young. Millions of pilgrims from around the world now visit Taizé annually to participate in the services and teachings, and the chants have spread worldwide. I remember singing one of the songs in the Upper Room in Jerusalem, when it spontaneously burst forth from a group of international tourists. Instantly the separate entourages of American, French, German, Dutch, Scandinavian, Japanese, and Russian pilgrims melded into a single voice chanting "Ubi caritas et amor, Deus ibi est" ("Where there is compassion and love, there God is found"). What a sign of hope for the human family!

Taizé chants (there are now well over a hundred of them) are easily available on CD or in small, inexpensive choir books.[12] "Worship in the style of Taizé"—simple services of chanting, meditation, scriptural readings, and often silent prayer—are catching on worldwide and represent a fascinating new hybrid: a kind of "fusion vespers" blending the heart of Christianity with the universal spirit of sacred chanting.

Songs of the Presence

But chanting can become even simpler than this; not even melodies and choir books are required. In traditional Sufi prayer, for example, a single word is chanted over and over—one of ninety-nine names (spiritual attributes) of God: "mercy," truth," "life," "peace," and so forth. With nothing but a single word, sometimes an accompanying drumbeat, and the conscious attention of the participants, a chant of enormous power and beauty rises in remembrance of God. Christians are by and large not used to chanting in this style. But that, too, is beginning to change. In wisdom circles throughout North America, a new form of chanting is emerging, featuring spontaneous improvisation on simple scriptural phrases. A growing repertory of chants called "songs of the presence" attests to the liveliness of this experiment. But the real product is not the songs, but in the process itself.[12]

We actually worked with this process at the beginning of the chapter when I asked you to create a simple chant from the Gospel of Thomas text, "Come into being as you pass away." As you put your voice behind the words and added a simple rhythm, you created a brand new "Song of the Presence." And you can do it whenever you want. Simply find any scriptural pith saying that appeals to you. It might be a line from a psalm—"Into your hands, I commend my spirit" (Psalm 31:5); "Deep calls to deep" (Psalm 42:9); "Taste and see that the Lord is good" (Psalm 34); or a line from the beatitudes, or any favorite teaching of the Wisdom Jesus: "Those who have ears, let them hear," "Abide in me as I in you," "Love one another as I have loved you."

The saying does not even have to be scriptural; you might want to use a line from a favorite poet—Rumi, Rilke, Mary Oliver—or a phrase from anywhere that has meaning to you. Whatever text you choose, the next step is to put your voice behind the words and begin to chant it, either in a monotone or a simple melody you make up yourself. (One of my friends talks about chant tunes "arriving.") If there are others who might join you (your meditation group?), you will have the thrill of hearing your little tune spontaneously burst into harmony, but in any case, it's yours to keep—or offer up. Chant it several times through as you enter your meditation or before your lectio divina—or just as well, in the car poking through traffic, as you jog or kayak, or in any of the myriad odd moments that life offers us for spiritual practice. Times and even traditions come and go, but presence is always the same. And the most powerful benefit of chanting is to bring you, heart and soul, into the beauty of that presence.

15

Welcoming

IN A WAY, it's a pity that Paul chose to introduce his beautiful kenotic hymn with the phrase, "Let the same mind be in you as was seen in Christ Jesus." When we hear the word "mind" we immediately think of some mental construct, and "putting on the mind of Christ" gets interpreted as "putting on the *attitude* of Christ." This in turn, is usually interpreted as trying to imitate those admirable qualities we see in Jesus's being: kindness, compassion, gentleness, integrity. But to copy these qualities without knowing where they come from in his being is not really putting on the mind of Christ; it's putting on the outer garments. To really put on the "mind" means we need to go deeper, discovering in our own selves the secret of Jesus's capacity to open himself to life in such an extraordinary way.

In this chapter I would like to explore a practice which, when used consistently and alertly, will allow us to do exactly that: to "put on the mind of Christ" by finding our way to the same inner alignment that enabled Jesus to do what he did, all the way up to and including embracing his own death. The practice was developed during the late 1980s by some of Thomas Keating's closest associates, and during the twenty years it has been taught and practiced within the Centering Prayer movement it has been known by a variety of names: "Open Mind, Open Heart Practice," "The Welcoming Practice," and currently "The Welcoming Prayer." It is somewhat nuanced in its applications and is often misunderstood, even by experienced practitioners. But when performed correctly, it demonstrates beyond all doubt that the kenosis Jesus taught and modeled, far from being passive or spiritually indifferent ("whatever . . ."), is in fact a pathway of vibrant spiritual strength and creativity connecting us to energetic fields far beyond our own finite resources. Through our willingness to work in the same way Jesus did, we are able to ground-truth his being in our own lives.

The practice is a three-step process of *acknowledging* what is going on internally during a distressing physical or emotional situation, "*welcoming*" it, and *letting it go*. Rather than being done at a specifically appointed daily time, it is a situational practice, intended for use in the midst of life whenever occasions of upset occur. Life being what it is, however, this pretty much equates to daily practice—sometimes several times daily.

Sensation, Sensation, Sensation

Before formally introducing the practice, I would like to invite you to a preliminary exercise. Put down this book for a moment, close your eyes, and picture yourself in a situation of stress. Say your job has just been terminated, or it's two in the morning and your teenager still is not home yet. Can you feel yourself inwardly tightening and bracing? Stay with that sensation for a minute or two, exploring how it actually feels in your body. Are your shoulders tense? Is your breathing fast and shallow? Your stomach churning? See if you can even deliberately intensify these sensations.

After a minute or so, consciously move in the opposite direction, still working directly with sensation. Un-brace, take a deep breath, and come down into your being. Soften inwardly. Open to the sensation of your own presence, and try to stay with that presence no matter what racket is going on in your mind. Keep returning consciously to that sensation of inner openness until you can feel a calmness beginning to return. If you are patient and firm, it eventually will. The aliveness of your "I AM" presence, sensed directly in this way, will eventually "trump" any mental or emotional turmoil that temporarily preempts it. Calm will return.

Congratulations! You have just done kenotic practice at the cellular level.

I realize that the exercise as I've structured it is a bit academic. Unless at this very moment you actually *are* waiting for that phone call from your missing teenager, it will be fairly easy to bring your unruffled being back into balance (it may be surprising to discover, however, that when real emergency hits, the instructions remain exactly the same). The real reason I introduced this visualization exercise is to give you right from the start a clear inner benchmark of the difference between working with an attitude and working with sensation. To work with this situation as an attitude might mean to pyschoanalyze yourself ("Why am I feeling so afraid?"), or to try to talk yourself out of your fear, or maybe even to say, "I let go of this fear and give it to Jesus." These are all ways of engaging the situation mentally. To work with sensation means to focus on the actual energy patterns the feelings and attitudes create in your body. Real kenotic work is done here—and, I believe, *only* here.

Once you understand the difference between sensation and attitude, it becomes possible to hear what is really being said in the most basic, no-frills statement of the kenotic path, which is as follows: *Never do anything in a state of internal brace—that is, in a state of physical tightness and resistance: you'll discover it's never worth the cost.*[1] This statement has nothing to do with giving up (that's an attitude) or relinquishing your right to defend yourself (also an attitude). At the sensation level the issue is simply this: in any life situation, confronted by an outer threat or opportunity, you have a choice between two options. You can either harden and brace defensively, or you can yield and soften internally. The first response will plunge you immediately into your small self, with its animal instincts and survival responses. The second will allow you to stay aligned with your heart, where the odds of a creative outcome are infinitely better.

Standing Firm or Caving In?

That state of spacious heart openness is known in spiritual tradition as *surrender*. Not what you usually think about when you hear the word "surrender," is it? We usually equate the word with capitulation and consider it a sign of weakness. But surrender, spiritually understood, has nothing to do with outer capitulation, with rolling over and playing dead. It has to do with keeping the right alignment inwardly that allows you stay in the flow of your deeper sustaining wisdom—to "feel the force," in those legendary words from the first *Star Wars* movie. In that state of openness you then *decide* what you're going to do about the outer situation. Whatever you do, whether you acquiesce or vigorously resist, your actions will be clear.

The seventeenth-century mystic Jacob Boehme had penetrated deeply into this realization when he wrote these words:

> Here, now, is the right place for you to wrestle before the divine face. If you remain firm, if you do not bend, you shall see and perceive great wonders. You will discover how Christ will storm the hell in you and will break your beasts.[2]

It is interesting how for Boehme "remain firm and do not bend" is the essence of surrender: exactly the opposite of how we usually use the term. He correctly realizes that surrender as a spiritual act requires "remaining firm"—but along the vertical axis of one's being, aligned with that deep heart-knowingness, rather than simply allowing oneself to be carried along in a stream of reactivity at the horizontal level. I learned this principle in my bones before I ever learned it in my mind through years of sailing on the Maine coast. It's always easy to run downwind, allowing the wind and sea to carry you along. But to make your way against the wind, you need a keel in the water and you need to stand firm on your heading. Surrender practice is exactly the same. Boehme further implies that this time of "wrestling before the divine face" is not just a test of spiritual willpower, but almost an alchemical breakthrough: in the moment of that struggle Christ mysteriously makes himself present and takes things the rest of the way. Surrender is not merely a means of restoring inner order but becomes a moment of direct encounter with the beloved master. If Boehme is right—and we will be keeping an eye on how this process might work—it gives us a huge clue as where to our own meeting ground with this ever-present master is most likely to be found.

The View from the Brain

Like all mystics, Boehme received his knowledge from direct revelation, and his insight echoes the teaching of all the great spiritual traditions: that surrender is an act of spiritual intelligence resulting in a markedly increased capacity for creative response. Recent discoveries in the field of neuroscience, however, have turned up striking physical evidence to support this ancient spiritual intuition. Since I am not myself a scientist, I am relying here on the work of such skilled interpreters as Sharon Begley, Joseph Chilton Pearce, and the HeartMath Institute.[3] Their publications can provide additional bibliography for readers interested in the more technical aspects of this discussion. But here is the gist of the emerging new picture, which I think you'll agree has profound implications for kenotic practice.

It is by now well known that the human brain is actually four-brains-in-one, built up sequentially over ten thousand years or more of evolution. Our primitive hindbrain (sometimes called our "reptilian brain") we share with our animal ancestors, and as with all animal brains, its primary concerns are the tasks of survival and self-defense. On top of and surrounding this ancient brain, nature has gradually built up three additional brains: the "old mammalian" or emotional-cognitive brain, the seat of our emotional intelligence; the neocortex, with its capacities for complex and creative thinking; and the prefrontal lobes, with their overall harmonizing and integrating effect and apparent deep entrainment with the electromagnetic field of the heart. Together, these form a human mind capable of a wide variety of creative and adaptive responses, including the capacity to receive what could be plausibly construed as "divine guidance."[4]

Now here is where the picture gets interesting. These interwoven brains are connected with each other (and with the heart) through complex neural pathways along a variety of possible routings. What neuroscience has been able to confirm is that any initial negative response to an outside stimulus immediately activates the reptilian brain, with its highly energized but extremely limited and archaic defensive maneuvers. In other words, any form of inner resistance or negativity (fear, anger, bracing) ensures that we are cut off from even our own higher human intelligence, let alone any remote possibility of divine assistance. The capacity to relax, soften, and open activates an entirely different neural pathway, allowing us to draw on a much greater range of our own creative intelligence—and even, it now increasingly appears, to engage those holographic capacities of heart perception we explored in chapter 3. Increasingly the technology is there to demonstrate that those ancient mystics were not merely spinning fantasies. Replace the old word "subtle" (as in "subtle faculties") with the new word "electromagnetic" (as in "electromagnetic resonance fields"), and the picture emerging from these two very different fields of knowledge becomes unnervingly congruent.

The Welcoming Practice

Within the Centering Prayer network the welcoming prayer is used mainly as an "attitude adjustment": a way of acknowledging God's presence in the midst of a distressing physical or emotional situation. Within a wisdom context, however, the wider possibilities of its ingenious methodology become apparent. Welcoming is intrinsically an energetic practice, geared to work at the level of sensation (not attitude), in order to actively imprint kenotic surrender as the innate first response to all life situations. Through its deliberate training in inner softening and opening, the practice begins to lay down new neural pathways in support of that deeper compassionate flow (call it your own higher intelligence or call it the Divine Mercy; perhaps they are not so different). Kenosis is experienced in (and through) the act of bringing oneself into a state of *unconditional presence*. In this more spacious spiritual state, the energy of being which might otherwise have been squandered in useless identified emotional reaction is recaptured and placed directly in the service of spiritual transformation.

The practice can be used both for emotional and physical upset. It can also be used on the other end of the pain-pleasure spectrum to confront "peacock feathers," as one of my spiritual teachers used to call them: those feelings of smug comfort or self-importance when the ego has managed to get exactly what it wants. But this is more subtle practice simply because you'll be less motivated to undertake it. Normally you begin with pain; it's easier to spot initially and you have more motivation to work with it.

The time to practice is as close as possible to the actual moment of the upset. Sometimes this is physically impossible (if you're in the midst of being verbally attacked, you may have to wait till the attack is over before you can practice); in that case, do it as soon after the event as possible, while the emotions or physical symptoms are still roiled up. The practice does take some actual physical time to do, particularly in the beginning while you're still learning the moves. As you get more experienced, the time required diminishes, until it can be done virtually simultaneously with the perceived upset itself.

Whether the situation is physical or emotional, the same three steps apply:

1. Focus or sink in
2. Welcome
3. Let go

Focus

To focus means to become physically aware of what's going on as sensation in your body. Exactly as we practiced in our introductory exercise, draw close to whatever is going on inside you. Whether it's physical pain or an emotion such as fear or anger, it will be expressed in the form of sensation. Pay attention to that. Is your chest tight? Breathing shallow or forced? Is your heart pounding?

Don't try to change anything. Just stay present. (In that first exercise we were deliberately trying to relax inner tightness, but only to get you used to working directly with sensation; it's not a part of the actual welcoming practice methodology.)

Do not—repeat: *do not*—use this occasion to analyze or justify yourself. Energetically, it's like pouring gasoline on a fire; the emotions will only flame higher. More important, from the point of the kenotic work we're up to, self-analysis locks you back into your egoic operating system with its constant stream of stories. The opportunity here is to go beyond that, into your larger self.

Taking time with this first step is important for a couple of reasons. First—as in all good biofeedback work—being consciously present to your body guarantees that you won't repress the emotion or dissociate from it (two perennial occupational hazards of the spiritual path). Second, it forces you to stay with sensation, which is where the work is going on anyway.

"Welcome"

This next step feels decidedly counterintuitive. Anchored there in the midst of all your upset, you begin to say, softly and gently, "Welcome, anger," or "Welcome fear," or "Welcome pain."

Why would you want to do a crazy thing like that? Isn't the point of this practice to get rid of that troublesome emotion or physical affliction?

No. The point is to not let it throw you out of presence. And the way—the only way—to do that is to wrap your deeper self around it through the power of your compassionate attention. Remember Rainer Maria Rilke's wonderful lines in *Letters to a Young Poet:* "Perhaps all the dragons in our lives are princesses who are only waiting to see us act, just once, with beauty and courage. Perhaps everything that frightens us is, in the deepest essence, something helpless that wants our love."[5] The energetic principle at stake is strong and clear. These "dragons" are energy knots in the stream of your awareness. When you beam the stronger power of your compassionate attention on them, they dissolve and melt back into the river.

I recommend naming them lightly, a point on which I am in some disagreement with the prevailing teaching in the Centering Prayer movement, which recommends only saying "welcome." But I have found that people will supply an object anyway, and nine times out of ten it will be the wrong object. "But incest is a hard thing to welcome, isn't it?" one woman asked me, unaware that what was on her plate in that moment was not incest but anger. Given the long and dangerous history in Christian spiritual practice of equating inner surrender with outer capitulation, it is important to keep reinforcing the point here. What you are welcoming is never an outer situation, only the feelings and sensations working within you in the moment. "*This* moment can always be endured," the well-known contemporary spiritual writer Gerald May reminds us,[6] and the act of welcoming roots us firmly in the now. Once we have endured and integrated what is on our plate internally, then what we do with the outer situation is for us to decide. Surrender means doing something out of the power of integrity, not knuckling under to coercion or abuse.

Let Go

The most important point I can make about this step is not to get to it too quickly. The work is really done in the first two steps, and this last one should be embraced only when you sense that the energy bound up in the upset is beginning to wane on its own. Then and only then you can use it like a coda in music: a final farewell when the movement has come to completion. Remember that letting go, too, is only for this moment. It is not a blanket vow never to be angry again, only a release of the anger in the present moment. Anger will almost certainly be back. But each time you are able to pass it through the light-beam of your compassionate attention, it loses more and more of its hold on your being.

When you do let go, there are two ways of going about it. The simplest is merely to say, "I let go of this anger" (or fear or pain), using the same word with which you named it before. But Mary Mrozowski, the actual founder of the method, preferred an unvarying litany:

> I let go my desire for security and survival.
> I let go my desire for esteem and affection.
> I let go my desire for power and control.
> I let go my desire to change the situation.[7]

Students of Thomas Keating's teachings will recognize these first three items as what he calls "the energy centers" of the false-self system.[8] Our core woundings in these areas, together with our misguided search for compensation, drive most of the unconscious behavior which is the source of our continuing human suffering. Mary liked to say, "I'm sending a strong message to the unconscious." The fourth item in this litany completely eliminates all doubt that one is "using" this practice to "fix" an undesirable situation. The goal is simply to stay present, at this deeper level "for the duration." Every moment of conscious presence actually takes place in eternity.

The Meeting Ground

Those steeped in Abraham Maslow's hierarchy of needs theory might shudder at the foregoing litany. How can one expect a person to entertain the notion of relinquishing these basic physical requirements? But wisdom practice has always known the deeper secret, beautifully expressed by Kabir Helminski in the following quotation: "Whoever makes all cares into a single care, the care for simply being present, will be relieved of all cares by that Presence, which is the creative power."[9]

With that realization, we penetrate right to the heart of the kenotic mystery, tingling in every cell of our body. It is not about giving up things we want or rolling over and playing dead. It is about connecting with an energy of sustenance so powerful and vibrant as it flows through our being from the infinite that all else pales in comparison. It not only flows through our being; it *is* our being.

There is a famous story from the Buddhist tradition, probably timeless but in its most recent renditions set during the Chinese invasion of Tibet. A soldier bursts into a monastery cell and thrusts his rifle into the belly of a meditating monk. The monk goes right on meditating. "You don't understand," says the soldier, a bit taken aback: "I have the power to take your life." The monk briefly opens his eyes and smiles sweetly at the soldier. "No, it's you who don't understand. I have the power to *let* you."

The power to let you . . . let it be . . . let be: the power of that *fiat* again. The core secret we are coming to understand is that the act of letting go, spiritually understood as *a cosmic energy exchange*, is the power by which Jesus could live and remain true to his path. It is the power through which he healed, the power through which he forgave, and the power through which he meets us now. Nor is it only *his* power, uniquely bestowed on him, as part of his prerogative as the only Son of God. That same power is hardwired into our own hearts and souls, and in that moment of complete surrender an explosion of presence goes off within us that is simultaneously an encounter with the wisdom master himself.

Life provides plenty of opportunities for this practice, to be sure. Sometime it seems as if that's what life is: "twenty-four/ seven" surrender immersion. The problem is, most of the time we don't catch ourselves when we "fall asleep," as it's called in wisdom work: when we brace and tighten and get thrown back into that smaller self. We go unconscious automatically. But if you stay alert and grounded in sensation and are willing to wake up as soon as you discover you've fallen into that place of tightness, then you can use all the adventures and misadventures life throws at you to strengthen and deepen your heart connection—and your Christ connection.

16

Eucharist

I T MAY SEEM curious to end our exploration of Christian wisdom practices with a discussion of the Eucharist, or Holy Communion, as it's more traditionally known. This ceremonial gathering of Christians at the altar rail to share bread and wine in memory of Jesus may not strike you as a spiritual practice so much as a cultic ritual. But my sense is that it began as a spiritual practice: that was Jesus's original intention. And to encounter it again in this context is to meet the wisdom Jesus head-on.

I have long maintained (and by no means with tongue in cheek) that my real qualification for being able to write about the Eucharist is my happy accident, now forty years ago, of having received my first Communion totally by chance. No joke! You may wonder in this day and age how that is possible, but remember that my childhood was lived in those extreme Protestant outposts of Christian Science and Quakerism. Neither of these is a liturgically oriented tradition, and I spent the first twenty years of my life in more-or-less-blissful ignorance that the whole world of sacrament and ritual even existed.[1]

The occasion of my unexpected initiation was a weekend trip with my college roommate to visit her boyfriend in London,

Ontario. I had become a passionate early music lover at that point, and so was totally thrilled to read a newspaper announcement that the famous boy choir from St. Paul's Cathedral in London, England, was going to perform in its namesake church the next morning. I dragged my roommate kicking and screaming, and it was a good thing I did. So enraptured was I by the music of the William Byrd *Mass* in *Four Voices* that I didn't even notice the long talking breaks between the movements. It was not till a very stern-looking usher stood right beside our row of pews and motioned us forward that I realized I was in a Communion line.

I was terrified, but the fear of displeasing this decidedly intimidating usher outweighed my fear of whatever awaited me ahead. My roommate, who'd been raised Catholic, whispered to me, "Just watch me and do what I do."

We approached the Communion rail, and following her, I knelt nervously. As a small round wafer was placed in my uplifted hands, she learned over and whispered, "Don't chew!" As the large silver chalice came by, she again leaned over and whispered. "Don't *touch* it." "How can I drink it then?" I started to ask, but she quickly hissed, "With your hands, I mean!" With those rudimentary instructions, I received my first Communion.

When our row uniformly rose from the altar rail, I was relieved to have survived. I started back to my pew thinking, "Well, that's that."

I was about two-thirds of the way back when I suddenly knew, "Well, that's *that!*" Quietly, not like some thunderous charismatic conversion, I simply knew that I had met my match; something utterly real, strangely compelling, strangely familiar, had entered my life that day—something I didn't even know I'd been missing but which for the first time made life feel really right. Even more impressive to me was the fact that *I knew* I knew this. Again, it was a moment of direct recognition, like in the snowfield so many years before when that golden voice had spoken to me. I was once again standing naked before the invincible certainty of my own heart.

What leads me to place so much weight on this experience is the fact that so far as I know, it came completely out of the blue. I was about as close to a pure heathen—or pure virgin—as they come: no preparation, no expectations, no catechism. I can only trust what my naked instincts told me: that this was a meeting—a direct encounter with a person who subsequently has never been seriously absent from my life. Long before I had absorbed any theology of memorial meals or sacrificial lambs, while I was still clueless about the subtle nuances of consubstantiation and transubstantiation, I knew the Eucharist as a place where I in my human form encountered the living Jesus in his subtle energetic form. That is what has stayed with me all these years and is still basically my touchstone as I keep working my way between the worlds.

What Was Jesus Up to That Night?

I have spoken frequently throughout this book about the hazards of "twenty-twenty hindsight," and nowhere is this blind spot in the Christian field of vision more evident than in our tendency to assume that Jesus's purpose here on earth was to found a new religion called Christianity. If you consciously or unconsciously buy into that assumption, it's almost impossible to avoid viewing the Last Supper through the rosy-colored glasses of sacramental theology. On the eve of his death, so the traditional churchly understanding goes, Jesus instituted the central ritual of the Christian church and "ordained" his eleven male disciples as its priests and apostles.

Virtually nothing could be farther from the truth. Whatever Jesus was up to during that night, founding a church was the last thing on his mind. What *was* on mind, seen from a wisdom perspective, was a whole lot more interesting.

In the past few years a great stir has been created by the publication of the Gospel of Judas from the Nag Hammadi collection.[2] Its sensational new claim is that Judas wasn't a traitor after all but was acting at the express behest of Jesus to set up the physical circumstances that would bring to fruition the cosmic act of salvation. The idea is rather like the old "O felix culpa"

("O happy fault") theology we looked at in chapter 8, only this time applied to Judas rather than Eve.

I didn't blink an eye through all the public uproar. I had already been introduced to this notion at least twenty years earlier through that inscrutable genius G. I. Gurdjieff. In his *Beelzebub's Tales to His Grandson*,[3] Gurdjieff claimed that Judas was indeed sent out to "buy time," leading the forces of the arresting armies on a wild goose chase so that Jesus would have time to complete with his remaining disciples special esoteric preparations essential to their continued work together. Realizing that the outer events of Holy Week were moving faster than he had anticipated, and seeing that the disciples were not yet spiritually prepared to stand on their own two feet in the Kingdom of Heaven, he opened up a classic "subtle body" channel between himself and them, using bread and wine as the specific vehicles of his presence.

In the surprisingly relevant language of modern computer programming, the bread and wine became an *instantiation,* "a specific instance," of his own resurrection body.[4] Through their intentional participation in this spiritual practice, the disciples could continue to "ingest" his energetic presence, and he could continue to teach them from "inside their own skins," at a subtle energetic level.

Remember logion 108 in the Gospel of Thomas: "Whoever drinks what flows from my mouth will become as I am, and I will become as he is, so that what is hidden may be manifest." That pretty much captures what Jesus was up to in the Last Supper. He would become a life growing within their own lives, the ombudsman of their own deepest selves, so that what was now obscured by fear and duality would ultimately be able to step forward in strength and oneness. Through his continued presence in their innermost beings, they, too, would become *ihidaya,* "single ones."

Gurdjieff's language around this idea is highly convoluted, but I have felt for twenty years now that the old rascal had a point here. Certainly his interpretation conformed to my own experience at the altar rail in Ontario that day. This sacramental sharing of the bread and wine in a conscious and intentional way is not primarily a "memorial meal" or a "proclaiming his death, until he comes again in glory" (1 Corinthians 11:26). That was Paul's theology, not Jesus's. Jesus was intent upon a living connection, an open channel that would allow him to remain in communion, across the energetic realms, with the hearts of his beloved ones—"I in you and you in me so that all may be one." The bread and wine, intentionally dedicated to that purpose, would be a pathway of *anamnesis,* or "living remembrance," through which his spiritualized personhood could continue to flow into them as living presence, blessing, and wisdom.

"When You Come into Your Kingdom . . ."

Remember that criminal on the cross from chapter 10? In the final moments of his life he uttered those extraordinary words: "Jesus remember me when you come into your kingdom"— to which Jesus responded, "Truly, this day you are with me in paradise."

For me, there is no simpler or better Eucharistic theology; that brief exchange captures the full mystical meaning of the practice. In all the great sacred traditions, the word "remembrance" is identical with "living presence." The criminal, recognizing who Jesus really is, asks to be "re-membered"—literally, "put back together again"—in that kingdom space. Jesus affirms that his very act of recognition *is* his translation into the kingdom, and the translation is instantaneous. In just this way, as one kneels today at the altar rail, it is not so much that Jesus "comes into" the bread and wine, as that we step through these sacred portals into the eternal banquet hall.

In the earliest days of Christianity, somehow this mystery was intuitively known. For its first two or three centuries, the church was flooded with unitive seeing, caught up in the dance of cosmic intimacy. Gratefully those early Christians participated in that one sacramental act Jesus had specifically charged them to do: to break bread and share the cup in living remembrance with him (not "*of* him"), extending their sense of felt immediacy to all time and space. And the church grew and spread like wildfire, propelled by an energy far beyond its own.

Gradually the excitement faded. Perhaps it had to. How long can one really keep alive this flame of living, burning, intimate connection to the realms beyond? In the fourth century Christianity was suddenly catapulted from a forbidden sect to the imperial religion. Some Christians fled into the deserts to keep alive the ancient practices by which they stayed connected to their living master. But the majority put their energies into building basilicas and hammering out creeds, and gradually, like a tide of ardor slowly receding from the world, Christianity was changed into a religion about Jesus rather than a religion *of* Jesus.

And of course, the cosmic meaning of the Eucharist shrank right along with this general contraction. To successive generations of Christians it would become, variously, a "memorial meal" (honoring a good but absent master), a "fellowship meal" (honoring that particular Christian community itself), an elaborate cultic ritual—and at its most primitive download, a kind of cultic magic, in which the bread and wine were separated from any notion of a remembrance meal and venerated as holy objects in their own right.[5]

And yet, beneath all the surface accretions and distortions, living water still flows. That accidental first Communion which forty years ago knocked me off my feet was the result of a direct connection with that still resonant reality, the reverberating reality of the "big bang" of Jesus's original intention. The failures of human vision and nerve can obscure this reality, but they cannot obliterate it altogether.

Jesus never asked anyone to form a church, ordain priests, develop elaborate rituals and institutional cultures, and splinter into denominations. His two great requests were that we "love one another as I have loved you" and that we share bread and wine together as an open channel of that interabiding love. I deeply regret the tendency so evident in the Roman Catholic Church these days, after forty years of remarkable ecumenical sharing and openness,[6] to once again to circle its wagons and restrict access to Communion to "card-carrying Catholics" only—that is, those in full conformance with the Roman Catholic magisterium. If these good bishops really trusted the Master they claim to believe in, rather than locking up the Eucharist in doctrinal prisons, they would follow Jesus's great counsel in his parable of the wedding feast (Matthew 22:1; Luke 14:15) and go out to the highways and byways and invite everyone in—so that Jesus himself could do the teaching "from the inside," in the manner that he himself inaugurated and sanctioned. From my own experience I can attest that he is fully capable of making his presence known.

It is not my place, of course, to challenge the survivalist mentality of an embattled power structure (only to point out once again how foreign this stance is to Jesus's kenotic path). Across the board in Christianity retrenchment seems to be in the air, as institutions fight for their lives and basic theological premises and established ways of doing things are in upheaval everywhere. I believe that this ferment is necessary and good; through it, Christianity will either grow into an appropriate form to match the consciousness of the twenty-first century, or else it will disappear as an institution and we will be left face to face with the naked presence of Christ—not such a bad option, when you come to think of it.

My concern is more for those of you who have begun to find your way into the wisdom stream, that in this time of institutional retrenchment you not be tempted to throw the baby out with the bathwater. As Ken Wilber helpfully points out in his *Integral Spirituality*, the same religious practice can look like a very different animal when articulated at different levels of human consciousness.[7] To date, most of the church's articulations of the Eucharist have been at lower levels of consciousness, in what Ken calls the "mythic" and "rational" range (you can return to chapter 3 to refresh yourself on these terms). But at heart the Eucharist is a wisdom practice originating from a nondual level of consciousness, and it is at that level that it truly comes into its own. When the bread and wine are directly seen as an instantiation—rather than either a consubstantiation or transubstantiation[8]—of the mystical body of Christ, we step through them into the living reality of interabiding love and meet the Wisdom Master face to face. Both our own eternal reality and his are never again in question. And we are able, more and more surely, to become "as he is," living our lives in the great flow of giving and receiving.

The word *Eucharist* literally means "thanksgiving." This is what the thanksgiving is all about.

Be patient! It will be some time yet before liturgies emerge above the radar screen that capture this wisdom understanding of Eucharist. But for all its constrictions and distortions at human hands, a genuine meeting place does still exist here: an exchange between the realms through which you will be nurtured and grow in your own wisdom journey. Eucharist is a core Christian practice. Search your local area for most the open, inclusive, and mystically attuned Christian community you can locate (or create), and partake as you can. And whether you find yourself on the road to Emmaus or the road to London, Ontario, may you come to meet the Wisdom Master (and your own true self) in the breaking of the bread.

Notes

Chapter 1. Jesus as a Recognition Event

1. Lynn Bauman, ed., *The Gospel of Thomas: Wisdom of the Twin* (Ashland, Ore.: White Cloud Press, 2004), p. 8.
2. A. H. Almaas, *Spacecruiser Inquiry: True Guidance for the Inner Journey* (Boston: Shambhala, 2002), p. 66.
3. Bruno Barnhart, *Second Simplicity: The Inner Shape of Christianity* (Mahwah, N.J.: Paulist Press, 1999), p. 48.
4. Unless otherwise noted, all translations are from the New Revised Standard Version of the Bible.
5. Barnhart, p. 49.
6. Ibid.

Chapter 2. Jesus in Context

1. For more on this fascinating subject see Ray Riegert and Thomas Moore, eds., *The Lost Sutras of Jesus: Unlocking the Wisdom of the Xian Monks* (Berkeley, Calif.: Seastone, 2003).
2. As, for example, in the flap stirred up in 2006 by the publication of the Gospel of Judas, one of the previously unpublished manuscripts within the Nag Hammadi collection. In direct contradiction to the canonical gospels, this text suggests that Judas had Jesus's blessing and full collaboration when he betrayed Jesus to the authorities following the Last Supper. The uproar among Christians was predictable.
3. Elaine Pagels discusses these two kinds of knowing at some length in *Beyond Belief: The Secret Gospel of Thomas* (New York: Random House, 2003), pp. 164–165. But since she is trained as a church historian rather than as a student of the Christian inner tradition, she stumbles over the word *epinoia,* explaining that "it has no precise

equivalent in English," and then tentatively offering "imagination." Those more familiar with the language of the Western theosophianic, or visionary, tradition would quickly amend her choice from "imagination" to "*imaginal*," meaning the capacity to perceive directly through images. As Arthur Versluis helpfully elucidates in his marvelous book *Wisdom's Children:* "By imagination the theosophers do not refer to 'fantasy.' Fantasy is daydreaming; fantasy has no discipline about it . . . By contrast, imagination refers to the science of images, to visionary inspiration by means of images. Imagination is not a matter of human creation, but of human perception" (Albany: State University of New York Press, 1999), p. 157. Through disciplined imagination, one can look directly into the invisible realms of reality: a necessary skill set for anyone who wishes to live in "Living Remembrance" with a living master who is yet invisible to earthly eyes.

4. For more on this subject, see my article "The Gift of Life: The Unified Solitude of the Desert Fathers" in *Parabola* 14, no. 2 (summer 1989), pp. 27–33. The article derives much of its substance from a more detailed study by my colleague and distinguished Syriac scholar Dr. Gabriele Winkler, particularly "The Origins and Idiosyncrasies of the Earliest Form of Asceticism," in *The Continuing Quest for God*, edited by William Skudlarek, OSB (Collegeville, Minn.: Liturgical Press, 1981).

5. The allusion here is to St. Paul's profound mystical hymn in Philippians 2:9–16, which he prefaces by saying, "You also should have the same mind in you as was in Christ." We will return to this mandate in some detail in chapter 3.

6. Some of the most significant (as well as personally authenticated) research on the Near Eastern roots of Jesus has been done by my friend and colleague Lynn Bauman, who unfortunately has not yet published his extensive findings. Bauman lived in Persia for more than a decade in the 1960s and worked intensively with the distinguished Islamic teacher Seyyed Hossein Nasr, now also in the United States. Through this intense immersion he was able to make sense of the Gospel of Thomas in a way that has yet, in my opinion, to be equaled by any other Western scholar. He sees in it, in incipient form, a teaching which would eventually come to its full articulation in the so-called Persian Platonism of the twelfth century. The three-thousand-year-old interweaving of strands between Jewish and Persian mysticism is, in Bauman's opinion, one of the major influences in Jesus's own emergence—and has continued long after his physical departure from the planet.

Chapter 3. "The Kingdom of Heaven Is within You"

1. Jim Marion, *Putting on the Mind of Christ* (Charlottesville, Va.: Hampton Roads, 2000).

2. The classic expression of this idea in Hindu teaching is "Atman is Brahmin": the realized Self is itself transcendent consciousness, the All.

3. The idea of levels of consciousness is a core building block of Wilber's philosophy and is set out in a number of his books over a two-decade time span, beginning with *Up from Eden* in 1986 and continuing through *Integral Spirituality* in 2006 (all books are Boston: Shambhala). During this time his ideas have inevitably evolved, and the schematic he now favors is somewhat different from the one Jim Marion was working with in 2000. The nine levels remain, but Wilber now prefers to identify them by color rather than descriptive title—a modification brought about the recent cross-fertilization between his own work and Spiral Dynamics. The "third tier" levels of consciousness that Marion refers to as "Subtle," "Causal," and "Non-dual" are now violet, ultraviolet, and clear light. The complete color chart can be found in *Integral Spirituality*, opposite p. 68.

4. For an excellent overview of current neuroscience and its implications for spiritual transformation, I am much indebted to my brother John K. Simmons, chairman of the Department of Religion at Western Illinois University, for sharing with me his paper "Neurotheology and Spiritual Transformation: Clues in the Work of Joel Goldsmith." The binary operator was first identified by the neurologists Andrew Newberg and Eugene D'Aquili as one of the two important cognitive operators within the brain. Its role is "to organize complex incoming stimuli into basic polar opposites." Their research entered the general public conversation as the cover story in the May 2001 issue of *Newsweek* magazine, called "God and the Brain: How We're Wired for Spirituality."

5. Kabir Helminski, *Living Presence: A Sufi Way to Mindfulness and the Essential Self* (New York: Jeremy Tarcher, 1992), p. 157.

6. This is Thomas Keating's preferred interpretation in his many teachings on Centering Prayer and the spiritual journey.

7. For this insight, I am indebted to Marcus Borg, who first offered it in conversation during a retreat we shared in Portland, Oregon, in January 2002. He develops it further in his book *The Heart of Christianity* (San Francisco: HarperSanFrancisco, 2003), p. 180.

Chapter 4. The Path of *Metanoia*

1. I owe this piece of data to Richard Rohr, who mentioned it during a conference we led jointly in Pembroke, Ontario, 3–5 May 2006. I believe his own source of information is the twentieth-century Roman Catholic theologian Karl Rahner.

2. Thomas Merton, "A Member of the Human Race," quoted from *A Thomas Merton Reader,* edited by Thomas McDonnell (New York: Image Books, 1996), p. 347.

3. Ken Wilber and Treya Killam Wilber, *Grace and Grit* (Boston: Shambhala, 1991), p. 401.

4. Antoine de Saint Exupery, *The Little Prince,* translated by Richard Howard (San Diego, Calif.: Harcourt, 1943).

5. Helen Luke, *Old Age* (New York: Parabola Books, 1987), p. 84.

6. Michael Brown, *The Presence Process* (Vancouver, B.C.: Namaste Publishing, 2005), p. 246.

7. *The Gospel of Thomas: Wisdom of the Twin,* translated and edited by Lynn C. Bauman (Ashland, Ore.: White Cloud, 2003), p. 145.

8. In the early 1990s Thomas Keating preached a series of sermons at St. Benedict's Monastery in Snowmass, Colorado, based on Scott's book and his own developing teaching on the False Self System. These were collected and edited to become *The Kingdom of God Is Like . . .* (New York: Crossroad, 1993), one of his most successful books.

9. One person who *did* see this is Fr. Joseph Chu-Cong, a Vietnamese-American Trappist monk whose delightful and relatively little-known book *The Contemplative Experience* I had the privilege of editing (New York: Crossroad, 1999). His chapter "Reading Scripture as Reading a Zen Koan" (pp. 46–50) first opened my eyes to this possibility.

10. Again like a good Zen master, Jesus demonstrates that assessing the strength of character and yearning in a prospective student is a key to transformation. Nicodemus is not ultimately thrown off by this rude introduction; something begins to ferment in him. We watch it slowly coming to fruit in his two subsequent appearances in the gospel: the first in John 7:50, when he tentatively but courageously attempts to stand up for Jesus in a dispute among the Pharisees, and again in John 19:39 when he steps forward to help bury the body of Jesus after the crucifixion.

Chapter 5. A Gospel of Thomas Sampler

1. Because the synoptic gospels (Matthew, Mark, and Luke) share so
   much overlapping material, biblical scholars have long posited that
   they depend on a common source, called "Q" (short for *Quelle,* the
   German word for "source"). This hypothetical missing source is
   generally seen to consist of a list of sayings and teachings of Jesus.
   The Gospel of Thomas certainly matches that job description.
   While it is probably not the official "Q" (as we shall see, it is tem-
   peramentally different from the synoptic gospels, much more in the
   flavor of Near Eastern spirituality), the fact that it is a list (without
   narrative elaboration) suggests that it is early: from the first stratum
   of Christian writings in the second half of the first century.
2. In compiling this sampler, I have drawn on two translations: Lynn
   Bauman's handsome critical edition, *The Gospel of Thomas: Wisdom
   of the Twin* (Ashland, Ore.: White Cloud, 2003), and an unpublished translation by Elaine Pagels that has been in my private collection for years. Logia 7 and 70 are from Pagels's translation; 22,
   42, 77, and 108 are from Bauman. The distinctions between them
   are mostly in style and nuance; only in 7 and 42 do the translations
   differ significantly, and only in 42 does this lead to a potentially
   significant difference in meaning.
3. Bauman's translation reads: "A lion eaten by a man is blessed as it
   changes into human form, but a human devoured by a lion is cursed
   as lion becomes human" (*Gospel of Thomas,* p. 19). The Coptic original translates literally as: "Blessed is the lion which becomes human
   when eaten by a man, but cursed is the man which a lion eats and the
   lion becomes human." Literally, then, the lion becomes human in
   both circumstances—but in very different ways. To my mind, however, Pagels's reversal of the terms in the second verse, while aca-
   demically less accurate, more pungently captures the real intention
   of the teaching: a point on which the Bauman edition concurs.
4. Quoted from Sara Sviri, *The Taste of Hidden Things* (Inverness,
   Calif.:Golden Sufi Center, 1997), p. 210.
5. Jacques Lusseyran, *And There Was Light* (New York: Parabola
   Books, 1998), p. 95.
6. This is one occasion where Bauman's translation and Pagels's differ significantly; Pagels's, the more literal of the two in this case,
   reads, "Be passersby." But what spiritual state is being alluded to in

the metaphor of a passerby? There is an obvious element of non-clinging to the horizontal axis. (This is a theme which Jesus also touches on strongly in his logion 21, where he describes his students in the following manner: "They are like little children living in a field not their own. When the owners of the field come and say, 'Give us back our field,' the children return it by simply stripping themselves and standing naked before them.") On the basis of the "synchronic resonance" among the sum total of these sayings, however, Bauman is probably correct in interpreting that Jesus is not simply calling for non-involvement; the attachment not squandered on the things of this world becomes the vital ingredient for creating "Being" in the larger realm. See Bauman, pp. 92–93.

Chapter 6. *Kenosis:* The Path of Self-Emptying Love

1. The version of this text I am citing here is a translation by the monks of New Camaldoli Hermitage, Big Sur, California, in active use in their liturgical and devotional life. It was through many years of singing this hymn with the monks during Saturday night vespers that its deeper significance began to open to me.

2. See Ken Wilber's insightful overview of the perennial philosophy in *The Eye of the Spirit* (Boston: Shambhala, 1997), and in particular, the following one-line summary in which the notion of spiritual ascent figures decisively: "The central claim of the perennial philosophy is that *men and women can grow and develop (or evolve) all the way up the hierarchy to Spirit itself,* therein to realize a "supreme identity" with Godhead—the ens perfectissimum toward which all growth and evolution yearns" (p. 39, italics Ken Wilber's). Note the emphasis on "up."

3. John of Sinai came to be known as John of the Ladder (John Klimakos in Greek, John Climacus in Latin) largely because of his principal work, *The Ladder of Divine Ascent.* The use of the ladder as a core metaphor for both "spiritual exercise" in general and lectio divina in particular became popular in the Christian West largely through an influential book *Scala Claustralium* (The Ladder of Monks), written by the twelfth-century Carthusian monk Guigo II. For an excellent discussion of this subject, see Simon Tugwell, OP, *Ways of Imperfection* (Springfield, Ill.: Templegate, 1985), particularly chapters 9, 10, and 11.

4. *Babette's Feast,* produced by Just Betzer and Bo Christensen, directed by Gabriel Axel, Panorama Films International, 1987.

5. Karl Rahner, "Thoughts on the Theology of Christmas," in *Theological Reflections*, vol. 3, *The Theology of the Spiritual Life* (New York: Seabury Press, 1974), p. 32. Rahner continues with the marvelous observation that "When God 'lets *himself* go outside of himself,' then there appears man."

6. Quoted from Kabir Helminski, *Living Presence* (New York: Putnam/Jeremy Tarcher, 1992), p. 142.

7. In his parable in Luke 12:13 (repeated in Thomas, logion 63) the wealthy man who builds a large storage barn as a hedge against the future dies before the night is over. The exception to this rule of "not counting the cost," as we saw in chapter 5, comes in those "hard teachings" in which the symbolic reference is not to material possessions but to inner wisdom which must be accumulated drop by drop from conscious experience.

8. These three great Cappadocian fathers are more commonly known in Christian tradition as monastics, not as founders of a wisdom school. But that is at least partially attributable to the fact that "wisdom school" is an unknown commodity in most of Christianity, and these Cappadocian monastics did indeed keep their more esoteric interests somewhat close to their chests. But my own repeated visits to the archeological remains of Cappadocian monasticism convince me that there is a good deal more esoteric wisdom here than meets the eye, reflected not only in the mystical theology but in the astonishing architecture, painting, and sacred geometry visible throughout. To say the very least, Cappadocia is one of those "thin places" where the visible and invisible realms intertwine closely, and its theologians were clearly proficient at perceiving the eternal unmanifest through the eye of the heart.

9. Raimon Panikkar, *Christophany* (Maryknoll, N.Y.: Orbis Books, 2004), p. 173.

10. Son of a Spanish Catholic mother and Hindu father, Panikkar has long been a pioneer in East-West dialogue. In *Christophany* (see note 9, above), he claims that the Trinity is in fact the symbol *par excellence* of Christian *advaita,* or non-dualism, expressing the concept "not one, not two, but both one and two." His work is a pioneering effort toward articulating Christian consciousness within a non-dual metaphysics. Richard Rohr and I teamed up to explore the "dance around" aspects of the trinity in a conference called "The Shape of God," sponsored by his Center for Action and Contemplation in Albuquerque, New Mexico, in January 2005. The lectures and discussions are available in CD, audiocassette, and VHS formats via the CAC website, www.radicalgrace.org.

11. Panikkar, p. 171.

12. Quoted from Lynn C. Bauman, ed., *A Book of Prayers* (Telephone, Tex.: Praxis Institute Press, 1999), p. 36.

Chapter 7. Jesus as Tantric Master

1. The synoptic gospels (Matthew, Mark, and Luke) offer variant expressions but the same bottom line—Matthew 3:14: "How is it that you come to me: I should be baptized by you!"; Mark 1:7–8: "After me comes one more powerful than I am; I have baptized you with water, but he will baptize you with the Holy Spirit. As for me, I am not worthy to bend down and untie his sandals"; Luke 3:16: "I baptize you with water, but the one who is coming will do much more: he will baptize you with the Holy Spirit and fire. As for me, I am not worthy to untie his sandals."

2. For an excellent and evenhanded treatment of the most flagrant of these distortions, see Karen King's *The Gospel of Mary of Magdala* (Santa Rosa, Calif.: Polebridge, 2003), particularly part 3: "The Gospel of Mary in Early Christianity."

3. As is perhaps less well known than it ought to be, Dan Brown's blockbuster *The Da Vinci Code* (New York: Doubleday, 2003) draws heavily on the research and hypothesis of an earlier book called *Holy Blood, Holy Grail*, by Michael Baigent, Richard Leigh, and Henry Lincoln (New York: Delacorte Press, 1982). At last hearing, this team of British journalists was considering a lawsuit against Brown for plagiarism, although considering the millions earned by his book, this might simply be simply be considered "the cost of doing business."

4. While all four gospels witness to her presence at or near the foot of the cross during the crucifixion, her presence is never mentioned during the Palm Sunday and Good Friday passion narratives of the Christian West, which instead direct their attention toward Peter's denial and subsequent remorse and reinforce the impression that Jesus died alone and abandoned. The first time I had ever seen her stunning witness portrayed liturgically was at a Good Friday post-Communion liturgy in Vézelay, France, during Holy Week 2005—and I can attest that it radically transformed my entire Christianity. I will have more to say about this in my forthcoming book on Mary Magdalene (Shambhala, 2009).

5. Margaret Starbird, *The Woman with the Alabaster Jar* (Santa Fe, N. Mex.: Bear and Company, 1993), pp. 50–51.

6. Both Luke (22:24) and Mark (10:41), however, mention an argument among the disciples as to which of them was the greatest.

7. I am quoting the opening of Dialogue 4 of the Gospel of Mary Magdalene from a new translation and critical edition in preparation by Lynn Bauman, Ward Bauman, and myself, which will include the Gospels of Thomas, Philip, and Mary Magdalene in a single volume titled *The Luminous Gospels* (Telephone, Tex.: Praxis Institute Press, 2009). The parallel passages are in King, p. 17, and Jean-Yves LeLoup, *The Gospel of Mary Magdalene* (Rochester, Vt.: Inner Traditions, 2002), p. 37.

8. From the Bauman, Bauman, and Bourgeault edition, end of Dialogue 3. The parallel passages are in King, p. 16, and LeLoup, p. 37.

9. Lynn C. Bauman, *The Gospel of Thomas: Wisdom of the Twin* (Ashland, Ore: White Cloud, 2003), p. 237.

10. From Bauman, Bauman, and Bourgeault edition, dialogue 2; parallel passages in King, pp. 14–15, and LeLoup, p. 29.

11. For a more extensive consideration of this issue, see my article "Reclaiming the Path of Erotic Love," in *Gnosis* 51 (spring 1999), pp. 43–48.

Chapter 8. The Incarnation

1. Quoted from the catechism in *The Book of Common Prayer of the Episcopal Church* (New York: Church Hymnal Corporation, 1977), p. 857.

2. Roberts alludes to this point in *The Path to No-Self* (Boston: Shambhala, 1985), p. 117, but develops it most fully in *What Is Self?* (Austin, Tex.: Mary Goens [privately published], 1989), pp. 200–202.

3. Karl Barth, *Christ and Adam: Man and Humanity in Romans 5* (New York: Harper and Brothers, 1957). Barth is perhaps the greatest theological giant of the twentieth century, stringent in his adherence to the classic dualisms of Western theology, yet illumined with great mystical insight.

4. This saying belongs to the Haddith Qudsi, or extra-Qur'anic revelation. When I say that the roots go down into perennial wisdom ground, I am referring to the Near Eastern wisdom traditions, which were Jesus's own primary formative ground and from which both Christianity and Islam would eventually emerge.

5. The former term, so named by the philosopher Arthur Lovejoy, is preferred by Ken Wilber; the latter is more prevalent in the Gurdjieff work. Both metaphors describe the same metaphysical map. For

an introductory overview, see Wilber, *The Eye of the Spirit* (Boston: Shambhala, 1997), particularly pp. 39–40.

6. *Meditations on the Tarot*, translated by Robert Powell (New York: Tarcher/Putnam, 2002), p. 33. The work was published anonymously, but the identity of its author has been indisputably established.

7. Here, too, the picture may be changing. A highly publicized article in a leading weekly news magazine a few years ago directly raised the question, "Does prayer work?" The evidence was strongly affirmative. For an eye-opening discussion of the "causal" energy of will and intention, see Lynne McTaggart, *The Field* (New York: HarperCollins, 2002).

8. Is our human plane in fact the endpoint? The wisdom cosmologies have tended to hedge their bets here. Virtually all the traditions acknowledge the existence of "sublunar realms," dominated by various forms of psychic hell. But it is not clear whether these realms are authentic evolutionary links in the great chain of being or simply aberrations of the earth plane. Gurdjieff—uniquely and perhaps with tongue in cheek—claims that the moon is not merely a planet, but a plane of consciousness lower than our own earth plane, which is "fed" by human unconsciousness. His quip, "Food for the moon!" was applied (often scathingly) to his fellow human beings who failed to develop their capacities of attention and consciousness, preferring to live entirely out of their habits and conditioning. Functionally, most wisdom cosmologies tend to place our human sphere at the bottom of the chain (or endpoint of the ray); from here, the direction is only "up."

9. Benedicta Ward, ed., *The Sayings of the Desert Fathers* (Kalamazoo, Mich.: Cistercian, 1984), p. 103.

Chapter 9. The Passion

1. *The Recapitulation of the Lord's Prayer*, pp. 88–89. This mystical gem was written anonymously and published privately by a twentieth-century British contemplative. According to the story told me when a copy was gifted to me, the author had been a student of the Russian philosopher P. D. Ouspensky and in attendance at Mr. Ouspensky's death. He was so moved by what he experienced during that passage that he lived as a hermit in India for three years seeking to go deeper into the mystery he had experienced.

2. These and the other miraculous events leading up to Israel's successful escape from Egypt are recorded in Exodus 12.

3. The 2004 Mel Gibson movie, *The Passion of the Christ*, is the latest in a long line of highly graphic spectacles intended to evoke personal agony, guilt, and devotion.

4. The word "Maundy" in fact comes from the Latin *mandatam*, or "mandate," referring to this New Commandment: "Love one another as I have loved you."

5. The Orthodox liturgy for vigils on Friday of Holy Week includes the reading of twelve passion accounts, including copious portions of the Farewell Discourses.

Chapter 10. Crucifixion and Its Aftermath

1. The NSRV version translates the last line in this excerpt as, "But this is your hour, and the power of darkness."

2. I am well aware of the "revised version" of this incident popularized in the recently published Gospel of Judas from the Nag Hammadi collection. Bart E. Ehrman, *The Lost Gospel of Judas* (New York: Oxford University Press, 2006). In this version Judas commits his "betrayal" under the explicit orders of Jesus in order to inaugurate the actions that will consummate the Paschal Mystery. I had in fact already been introduced to much this same idea by G. I. Gurdjieff, who more than sixty years ago had argued in his *Beelzebub's Tales to His Grandson* (reprint, New York: Viking Arkana, 1992) that Judas was deliberately sent out as a decoy in order to buy time for Jesus to complete his final instructions with the remaining disciples—specifically the Last Supper, which Gurdjieff saw not as a memorial meal but as a specific esoteric ritual that would set in place the energetic channels through which Jesus might continue to teach the apostles after his departure from the flesh. I think there is much merit in this suggestion, and I will return to it in my final chapter on the Eucharist. On the whole, however, I find the traditional portrait of Judas as a Zealot to be both the more historically likely and the more psychologically plausible.

3. If we follow the account from the Gospel of John, it could well have been the footwashing ceremony, which immediately precedes Judas's departure from the supper table. Here Jesus's dramatic enactment of his teaching that the master is the one who serves, and his instruction "You must wash one another's feet" (John 13:14) would certainly have dashed Judas's hopes of a messianic king ruling in glory.

4. That most brilliant of all Christian mystics, Meister Eckhart, suggests

that it is in fact a "both/and" scenario: both responses were playing out in Jesus but at different levels of his being. In his Sermon Twenty-four, commenting on the gospel passage (Matthew 26:38; Mark 14:34) that depicts Jesus saying, "My soul is sorrowful unto death," Eckhart elucidates: "Christ, however, always remained united to the Highest Good, as a person of the Trinity. He never lost sight of his power; he enjoyed the same nearness and union with the Father and the Holy Spirit even during the height of his sufferings. No sorrow or pain or death could affect this union. Indeed, even when Christ's physical body died a painful death on the cross, his noble spirit lived in contemplation of the Highest Good. In view of this sphere, however, in which his noble spirit was related to the senses and united with his holy body, inasmuch as our Lord called his created spirit a soul, insofar as it was the life principle of the body, and inasmuch as it was united to the sense and the mind, to this manner and degree his soul was 'sad under death' for his body to die." Quoted from Matthew Fox, *Breakthrough: Meister Eckhart's Creation Spirituality in New Translation* (New York: Image Books, 1980), p. 342.

5. The traditional gospel designation for these two persons is thieves. But modern biblical scholarship has established with virtual certainty that they were in fact political criminals—the same charge as was laid upon Jesus.

6. I will develop this point in much greater detail in my forthcoming book on Mary Magdalene (Shambhala, 2009).

7. For an extensive and mystically brilliant discussion of this point, see Ladislaus Boros, *The Mystery of Death* (New York: Herder and Herder, 1965; reissued in paperback, New York: Seabury Press, 1973), particularly his comments on pp. 147–149. Boros earlier in the same volume describes how in death a human soul becomes "pan-cosmic"—i.e., "given access to a more really essential proximity to matter" (p. 77). Applying this same insight to Jesus's death, he concludes: "Christ's human soul in death would have entered into an open, concrete, ontological relationship with the universe. This means that the cosmos in totality would have become the bodily instrument of Christ's humanity . . . When, in the way we have just explained, Christ's human reality was planted, in death, right at the heart of the world, within the deepest stratum of the universe, the stratum that unites at root bottom all that the world is, at that moment in his bodily humanity he became the real ontological ground of a new universal scheme of salvation embracing the whole world" (p. 149).

8. Annie Dillard, *Pilgrim at Tinker Creek* (New York: Bantam Books, 1974), p. 184.

9. Jacob Boehme, *The Way to Christ,* edited by Peter Erb (Mahwah, N.J.: Paulist Press, 1978), p. 179.

10. The poem was printed on the face of a small greeting card given to me by a British hermit friend. I know that it hails from the order known as the Sisters of the Love of God, but have been unable to further identify its author.

Chapter 11. The Great Easter Fast

1. I must confess I have always found this "birthday of the church" idea somewhat distasteful, not simply because of the excesses to which it is often carried in parish celebrations (birthday cakes, balloons, and the like), but because of its extraordinarily anachronistic theology. It assumes that the purpose of Jesus's earthly sojourn was to found a religion known as Christianity, for which his male disciples were being trained and commissioned as priests. While these ideas are still deeply ensconced in Christian self-understanding, they are almost entirely at variance with the findings of modern biblical scholarship and are a major stumbling block in the church's relationship with the wisdom tradition, with women, and with other members of the family of world religions. For a penetrating analysis, see Karen King, *The Gospel of Mary of Magdala* (Santa Rosa, Calif: Polebridge, 2003), particularly her final chapter, "The History of Christianity."

2. For an excellent introduction to the principle of *ascesis* (asceticism) as athletic training, see Kyriacos Markides, *Riding with the Lion* (New York: Viking Penguin, 1994), particularly pp. 282–283. Kabir Helminski presents a helpful discussion of the Sufi perspective on fasting in his *The Knowing Heart* (Boston: Shambhala, 1999). On p. 74 he makes the striking observation: "Another cure for the heart is keeping one's stomach empty. An excess of food hardens the heart." I discuss the relationship between asceticism and spiritual transformation in my article "The Gift of Life: The Unified Solitude of the Desert Fathers," *Parabola* 14, no. 2 (summer 1989), pp. 27–35.

3. The original version of Mark ends with the Maries' terrified discovery of the empty tomb and does not deal with the resurrection at all. The present concluding paragraphs (Mark 16:9–20) are thought by most scholars to have been added on later and seem to reflect the influence of Luke-Acts.

4. The appearance recorded in Luke 24:33–25:43 probably recounts

the same episode as John 20:19. Although in Luke's account Thomas does not figure in the dialogue, there is an identical emphasis on the full physicality of Jesus's presence, as Jesus asks the disciples, "Have you anything to eat?" and consumes a piece of boiled flesh before their eyes. Luke also mentions (24:34) a report of an appearance to Simon, but this is neither enacted nor confirmed in the other gospel accounts. Matthew places Jesus's final gathering with the disciples in Galilee, but on a mountain rather than by the Sea of Tiberias.

5. Valentin Tomberg, *Meditations on the Tarot*, p. 574.

6. The gospel of John refers several times to a person who is specifically singled out as "the beloved disciple." Traditionally this person has been thought to be John himself, but in the light of the recent *Holy Blood, Holy Grail*–fueled reappraisals (Michael Baigent, Richard Leigh, and Henry Lincoln, *Holy Blood, Holy Grail*, New York: Delacorte Press, 1982), several new candidates have emerged, including Lazarus and Mary Magdalene herself. Since the point I am making does not require venturing into these turbulent seas, I will for the moment stick with the traditional ascription.

7. Murat Yagan, a contemporary spiritual master in both the Sufi and Christian lineages, in fact claims that the real esoteric meaning of "dying before you die" is to become capable of "visiting at will the Abode which awaits you after death." Through this conscious travel between the realms, not only does one develop personal trust in the vastness and goodness of the Divine Compassion, but one becomes a viaduct for these spiritual qualities, carrying them back into the earth realm to the benefit of all humankind. For a remarkable interview with Yagan on exactly these points, see "Sufism and the Source" in *Gnosis* magazine, no. 50 (winter 1994), pp. 40–51.

8. Once again I call attention to Ladislaus Boros's remarkable book, *The Mystery of Death* (New York: Herder and Herder, 1965; reissued in paperback, New York: Seabury Press, 1973). In endnote 7 in chapter 10 I quoted his comment on the cosmic "sea change" effected in the moment of Christ's death. Here I will add his teachings on Christ's ascended state: "Christ's transfigured body is the archetype of the universe as already introduced in a mysterious and hidden way into the state of transfiguration . . . It is also the essence of our bodily contact with Christ. Free of all 'fleshly' constraints of time and place, Christ is able to reach the men of all times and places and make them members of his transfigured body; i.e., enable them to participate in his 'pneumatic' corporeity . . . Descent into the interior of all visible creation, and resurrection as an entry into the pneumatic openness

of the corporeal are, therefore, two reciprocally interpenetrating aspects of the one passage of Christ through death" (p. 157).

9. I have phrased my statement in this way in order to avoid the implication that all persons at a certain level of spiritual attainment will meet Jesus Christ. While many Christians make that claim, I find it to be not only unsubstantiable, but also spiritually imperialistic. I would expect that a Buddhist at that same spiritual level would more likely meet the Buddha, a Muslim Mohammed, and so forth—although remarkable exceptions do occur. My own take is that there is always a feedback loop between the universality of divine being and the concepts and archetypes through which a particular spiritual tradition expresses itself. Rather than claiming that all human beings will meet Christ (and recognize him as such), I would merely want to say that the meeting with Christ, whenever and to whomever it occurs, is an ultimate encounter. Not "more" ultimate or "less" ultimate than a parallel encounter on a different spiritual path, but *that same ultimacy* clad in the language and form most congenial to that particular believer.

10. I was first introduced to this poem by Fr. Curtis Almquist, SSJE, at a clergy conference of the Episcopal Diocese of Colorado in May 1997. I have continued to use the translation he gave to us and have been unable to substantiate its source.

11. We usually use the term to refer to our personal interior world. In the inner traditions, the term is more appropriately applied to the view that ensues when the subject/object dualism has been transcended—in other words, from non-duality. For a technical but extremely helpful discussion of this point, see Raimon Panikkar, *Christophany* (Maryknoll, N.Y.: Orbis, 2004), pp. 67–71.

Chapter 12. Centering Prayer Meditation

1. The two most widely recognized teachers associated with centering prayer are Fr. Thomas Keating and Fr. Basil Pennington, both of whom were among the original architects of this practice when it was first introduced at St. Joseph's Abbey in Spencer, Massachusetts, in the early 1970s. Their numerous books are easily available online. In 1983 Fr. Keating founded Contemplative Outreach, an organization dedicated to providing resources and support for lay contemplatives. The organization offers regular Centering Prayer retreats at all levels and provides a considerable inventory of books, CDs, and videos by Fr. Keating and an emerging crop of protégés.

The website can be accessed at www.contemplativeoutreach.org; the office phone number (in Butler, New Jersey) is 973-838-3384. My own book, *Centering Prayer and Inner Awakening* (Boston: Cowley, 2004) contains an extensive bibliography of works by Frs. Keating and Pennington.

2. Ira Progoff, ed., *The Cloud of Unknowing* (New York: Delta Books, 1957), p. 76.

3. In Centering Prayer terminology, the word "thought" is used in the broadest possible way to cover any sense perceptions at all. It includes not only mental activity, but also bodily sensations, feelings, reflections, memories, images, and spiritual experiences: anything that breaks the open, diffuse awareness and creates a focal point for the attention.

4. Unless, of course, you have mastered lotus position and prefer meditating on a cushion and mat, Eastern style. If that is the case, you are perfectly free to continue meditating in that posture. Most Westerners will probably be drawn to a chair, however (at least initially), and in this position it is very important to un-learn that classic cultural habit of crossing one's legs; it definitely impedes the free flow of energy through your body. If you are short, a cushion or even a thick book tucked beneath your feet helps to keep your knees comfortably horizontal.

5. Fr. Keating advises strongly that meditation for longer than two hours a day needs to be under the supervision of an experienced guide in order to help integrate unconscious material or psychic energies that may be stirred up through intensive meditation. Except in situations where there is a history of psychosis or extreme trauma, meditating within the prescribed forty minutes to an hour daily is perfectly safe.

Chapter 13. *Lectio Divina*

1. I am primarily using the translation from the Episcopal Book of Common Prayer (New York: Church Publishing Company, 1977), p. 785, which I admire for its simplicity and elegance. This translation however, leaves out the word "weaned" (it only states "like a child upon its mother's breast"). I have reinserted it here not only for the sake of textual accuracy, but also because it conveys the essence of the child's disposition: no longer hungrily feeding, but merely resting contentedly.

2. For an elegant treasure trove of these Old Testament wisdom texts, beautifully set up for lectio divina, see Rami Shapiro's *The Divine Feminine in Biblical Wisdom Literature* (Woodstock, Vt.: SkyLight Paths, 2005).

3. Philip Booth, "Heading Out," in *Selves* (New York: Penguin Books, 1990), p. 28.

4. For a brief overview of the traditional monastic teachings on the "four senses of scripture"—that is, the emergence of progressively more subtle and integrated ways of hearing—see my *The Wisdom Way of Knowing* (San Francisco: JosseyBass, 2003), pp. 93–96.

Chapter 14. Chanting and Psalmody

1. For an excellent and accessible introduction to this abstruse field, see Brian Greene, *The Elegant Universe* (New York: Vintage Books, 1999).

2. The Latin language, with its abundance of "ah" and "oh" vowels, seems to have a particular corner on this market: one of the reasons, I believe, that people intuitively recognize the Roman Catholic mass and liturgical psalmody as sounding "more sacred and mysterious" when performed in Latin.

3. In the sixth-century *Rule of St. Benedict,* which laid the basic foundations for monastic practice in the West, Benedict comments that monks who in a week's time say less than the full 150 psalms "betray extreme indolence and lack of devotion in their service. We read, after all, that our holy fathers, energetic as they were, did all this in a single day." *The Rule of St. Benedict* (Collegeville, Minn.: Liturgical Press, 1980), p. 215.

4. *The Sayings of the Desert Fathers,* translated by Benedicta Ward (Kalamazoo, Mich.: Cistercian, 1984), p. 64.

5. See endnote 3, above. Benedict's instructions on liturgical psalmody occupy thirteen of the Rule's seventy-three chapters.

6. In the Byzantine world, the foundations of monastic liturgical chanting were laid by St. Basil the Great (329–379), one of the celebrated Cappadocian fathers and the great patriarch of monasticism in the Christian East.

7. Judith Sutera, *The Work of God* (Collegeville, Minn.: Liturgical Press, 1999).

8. The most important single resource bank for Christian sacred chanting is the Chicago-based GIA Publications. This Roman Catholic but ecumenically oriented publishing house provides scores and

recordings for virtually all aspects of the Western chant tradition, from Gregorian to Taizé (see ahead in the text), including wonderful, singable psalm tones for both individual and group use. The website is www.giamusic.com; phone 800-442-1358.

9. A name colloquially given to a number of psalms marked by violent imprecations hurled against the enemy. Psalm 109 is the most notorious, but these periodic violent outbursts occur throughout the psalms.

10. *John Cassian: Conferences,* translated by Colm Luibheid (Mahwah, N.J.: Paulist Press, 1985), p. 133.

11. The monks continue to use traditional psalmody in their private community worship.

12. CDs are available from the Praxis Institute for Research and Learning in Elwood, Texas. The website is www.praxisofprayer.com.

Chapter 15. Welcoming

1. For this insight I am indebted to the Edmonton guru John deRuiter, who first presented the notion during a retreat held 20–22 April 2000.

2. Jacob Boehme, *The Way to Christ* (Mahwah, N.J.: Paulist Press, 1978), p. 240.

3. Sharon Begley, *Train Your Mind, Change Your Brain* (New York: Ballantine, 2007); Joseph Chilton Pearce, *The Biology of Transcendence* (Rochester, Vt.: Inner Traditions, 2004). Begley is a science columnist for the *Wall Street Journal* and has worked closely with the Dalai Lama (he contributed the Foreword) on his international Mind Life Conferences. These conferences are part of a continuing effort to establish a top-quality dialogue between classic meditation disciplines and the findings of modern neuroscience. Pearce's book is one of my personal favorites, the unique synthesis of a brilliant mind and profound spiritual insight. His book draws extensively on the work of the California-based HeartMath Institute and, while not as objective as Begley's, is filled with stunning intuitive leaps that bring the big picture together in a compelling way. Pearce is also a lifelong disciple of the Wisdom Jesus, and his insights in this regard are as valuable a part of the book as his scientific data.

4. Among these aforementioned leaps in *The Biology of Transcendence,* none is more intriguing for me than Pearce's suggestion that the heart, with its huge toroid-shaped electromagnetic field, is a "frequency generator" (p. 68), drawing from electromagnetic fields

both within and beyond our known space time to "create the fields of information out of which we build our experiences of ourselves and the world." He further speculates that "our heart is an instrument or representative of the universal heart" (p. 66), and that "our brain and body are the manifestation of the universal heart's diversity, or individual expression. Brain and body are fashioned to translate from the heart's frequency field information for building up our unique, individual world experience" (p. 66). These insights accord well with the wisdom insight that the heart is in some sense a hologram of the divine heart, and in that sense is a channel for an energy and coherence of being beyond the boundaries of our individual selfhood. Through our heart we are connected to all hearts and receive the guiding pattern and energy of the whole.

5. Rainer Maria Rilke, *Letters to a Young Poet* (Boston: Shambhala, 1993), p. 101.

6. Gerald May, *Will and Spirit: A Contemplative Psychology* (San Francisco: Harper and Row, 1982), pp. 197–199.

7. For more on Mary Mrozowski and her compelling journey to spiritual mastery, see my *Centering Prayer and Inner Awakening* (Boston: Conley, 2004), Chapter 13.

8. For an overview of this teaching and additional bibliography, see my *Centering Prayer and Inner Awakening* (Boston: Cowley, 2004), particularly chapters 9 and 13. Thomas Keating's most extensive treatment of the false-self system can be found in his *Invitation to Love* (Rockport, Mass.: Element, 1992).

9. Kabir Helminski, *Living Presence: A Sufi Way to Mindfulness and the Essential Self* (New York: Jeremy Tarcher/Putnam, 1992), p. 26.

Chapter 16. Eucharist

1. Christian Scientists do in fact celebrate monthly communion of the individual-wafer-and tiny-glass-of-grape-juice variety typical of many Protestant denominations. But this practice was never open to those still in Sunday school, and I had left the Christian Science fold long before I graduated from Sunday school.

2. Bart E. Ehrman, *The Lost Gospel of Judas* (New York: Oxford University Press, 2006).

3. G. I. Gurdjieff, *Beelzebub's Tales to His Grandson* (New York: Viking Arkana, 1992), pp. 676–679.

4. For this insight I am grateful to John Hiestand, a computer programmer and now a student at the Northwest Theological Consortium,

who developed this idea in a research paper called "The Object-Oriented God," which he graciously shared with me in September 2007.

5. In many parts of the Christian world the practice still remains in effect of venerating the monstrance: a large, transparent receptacle in which the consecrated bread (the host) is displayed to the multitudes. The custom of venerating the reserve sacrament (consecrated bread and sometimes wine set aside in a special tabernacle after communion) looks on the surface to be a similar "magical practice," but many Christians claim (and I myself have experienced) that there is palpable energy emanating from the tabernacle. My own preference is to see this "force field" as residing not so much in the objects themselves as in the energy of intention that they bear. But however one interprets it, the energy is sufficiently perceptible to suggest caution in simply labeling this practice "magical."

6. This new spirit of openness and inclusivity was one of the most powerful fruits of that remarkable Vatican II church council, convened by Pope John XXIII during the early 1960s.

7. Ken Wilber, *Integral Spirituality* (Boston: Shambhala, 2006), pp. 183–186. Wilber calls this "The Level/Line Fallacy": "the confusing of a level of a line [i.e., the degree of conscious development and articulation at any given stage] with the line itself."

8. These traditional theological categories describe different scenarios of how Christ is present in Eucharist. In *transubstantiation* (the traditional Roman Catholic position), the bread and wine are literally changed into the body and blood of Christ. In *consubstantiation* (favored by most Protestant interpretations), Jesus becomes present with and to the congregation through the offering up of the Eucharist itself; there is less emphasis on pinpointing the precise moment in which the transformation of substance occurs. To my mind, both of these traditional sacramental theologies are looking at the picture backward: the issue is not so much how Jesus enters time and form as how we ourselves are transported beyond it. The new model of instantiation offers a helpful resolution to this dilemma, suggesting that as in all holographic reality, the process is instantaneous and completely reciprocal since, at root, the whole and the part can never be separated from one another.

Selected Reading

Amis, Robin. *A Different Christianity*. Albany, N.Y.: SUNY Press, 1995. An eye-opening guide to the Christian inner tradition, particularly as it has emerged through the Orthodox lineage of Mount Athos.

Baldock, John. *The Alternative Gospel: The Hidden Teachings of Jesus*. Boston: Element Books, 1997. Important resources for re-visioning Jesus as a master of wisdom.

Barnhart, Bruno. *The Good Wine: Reading John from the Center*. Mahwah, N.J.: Paulist Press, 1993. A profound commentary on the Gospel of John by a contemporary monk and contemplative master.

———. *Second Simplicity: The Inner Shape of Christianity*. Mahwah, N.J.: Paulist Press, 1999. A poetic and insightful exploration of the loss and reemergence of Christian unitive wisdom.

Bauman, Lynn. *The Gospel of Thomas: Wisdom of the Twin*. Ashland, Ore.: White Cloud Press, 2003. An important new translation of this primary source for Jesus's wisdom teaching, including notes and questions for reflection in a format highly conducive to group study.

Borg, Marcus. *The Heart of Christianity: Rediscovering a Life of Faith*. San Francisco, Calif.: HarperCollins, 2003. A highly readable introduction to the emerging "new paradigm" (that is, wisdom paradigm) within Christianity by a distinguished contemporary scholar and teacher.

Boros, Ladislaus. *The Mystery of Death*. New York: Herder and Herder, 1965; reissued in paperback, New York: Seabury Press, 1973. An extraordinary journey through the Christian Paschal Mystery, based on the seminal insight that the moment of death gives human beings the opportunity to make their first fully free and conscious choice. This is a work of pure mystical revelation, difficult but breathtaking.

Bourgeault, Cynthia. *Centering Prayer and Inner Awakening*. Boston, Mass.: Cowley, 2004. A complete guidebook to the theory and practice of Centering Prayer.

————. *Chanting the Psalms.* Boston, Mass.: Shambhala, 2006. A comprehensive introduction to Christian sacred chanting, including an instructional CD.

————. "The Gift of Life: the Unified Solitude of the Desert Fathers." *Parabola* 14, no. 2 (1989), pp. 27–35. The Desert Fathers from a wisdom perspective, together with an exploration of how this perspective was lost.

————. *Mystical Hope: Trusting in the Mercy of God.* Boston, Mass.: Cowley, 2001. A new look at Christian metaphysics from a wisdom perspective.

————. *The Wisdom Way of Knowing.* San Francisco, Calif.: JosseyBass, 2003. An accessible and practice-oriented introduction to the Christian wisdom tradition.

Brock, Sebastian, ed. *The Syriac Fathers on Prayer and the Spiritual Life.* Kalamazoo, Mich.: Cistercian, 1987. An important sourcebook for the wisdom tradition in early Christianity.

Casey, Michael. *Sacred Reading: The Ancient Art of Lectio Divina.* Liguori, Mo.: Liguori/Triumph, 1996. An excellent practical guide to lectio divina by a contemporary Trappist abbot.

Chu-Cong, Joseph, OCSO. *The Contemplative Experience: Erotic Love and Spiritual Union.* New York: Crossroad, 1999. A luminous exploration of Christian monastic love mysticism as a kenotic path, with particularly helpful chapters on the Eucharist and lectio divina.

Clément, Olivier. *The Roots of Christian Mysticism.* Hyde Park, N.Y.: New City, 1993. A foundational study of visionary seeing and the metaphysics of *theosis* (the divinization of the human person) and *theophany* (the radiant presence of God) in the first five centuries of Christian thought. Clément demonstrates chapter-and-verse how contemporary Christian theology actually represents an impoverishment of the original Christian integrative wisdom.

Cousins, Ewert H. *Christ of the Twenty-first Century.* Rockport, Mass.: Element Books, 1992. A groundbreaking effort to liberate Christ from the cultural conditioning of an overly institutionalized and Westernized Christianity and to establish the baselines for an authentic interspiritual sharing.

Ehrman, Bart. *Lost Christianities: The Battle for Scripture and the Faiths We Never Knew.* New York: Oxford University Press, 2003. A brilliant study of the pluralistic beginnings of Christianity by a well-known New Testament scholar.

————. *Lost Scriptures: Books That Did Not Make It into the New Testament.* New York: Oxford University Press, 2003. A helpful and balanced introduction to the core texts of the Christian wisdom tradition.

Freeman, Laurence. *Jesus: The Teacher Within.* New York and London: Continuum, 2000. An intimate and insightful exploration of the Wisdom Jesus by a leading contemporary contemplative and founder of the World Community for Christian Meditation.

Hall, Thelma. *Too Deep for Words: Rediscovering Lectio Divina.* Mahwah, N.J.: Paulist Press, 1988. The classic introduction to the practice of lectio divina, written specifically for contemporary lay contemplatives.

Keating, Thomas. *Awakenings.* New York: Crossroad, 1990. A collection of homilies on the parables, based on the scholarly work of Bernard Brandon Scott. Followed by *Reawakenings* (Crossroad, 1993) and *The Kingdom of God Is Like . . .* (Crossroad, 1993).

————. *The Mystery of Christ.* Rockport, Mass.: Element, 1987. An exploration of Christian liturgy and the liturgical year as a mystical participation in the life of Christ.

————. *Open Mind, Open Heart.* Rockport, Mass.: Element Books, 1986. The classic introduction to the practice of Centering Prayer by a contemporary contemplative master.

Kelly, J. N. D. *Early Christian Doctrines.* New York: Harper and Row, 1960. The classic introductory textbook to the foundations of Christian orthodoxy.

King, Karen L. *The Gospel of Mary of Magdala: Jesus and the First Woman Apostle.* Santa Rosa, Calif.: Polebridge, 2003. An excellent translation and commentary by an outstanding contemporary scholar. The concluding chapter, "The History of Christianity," should be required reading for all Christians. It builds a brilliant case for the pluralistic beginnings of Christianity and the hazards of misusing the label "gnosticism" as a means of judging deviation from an "orthodoxy" which in fact did not exist for the first three centuries of Christian life.

LeLoup, Jean-Yves. *The Gospel of Mary Magdalene.* Rochester, Vt.: Inner Traditions, 2002. *The Gospel of Philip.* Rochester Vt.: Inner Traditions, 2004. *The Gospel of Thomas.* Rochester, Vt.: Inner Traditions, 2005. Three core texts of the Christian wisdom canon, presented by an outstanding contemporary mystic. While LeLoup's

translations need to be carefully backstopped for accuracy, his intimate knowledge of the visionary realms provides the springboard
for his brilliant and bold intuitive leaps. The commentaries intertwined with these translations are a veritable feast of Christian esoteric wisdom.

——. *The Sacred Embrace of Jesus and Mary.* Rochester, Vt.: Inner
Traditions, 2005. A courageous and insightful introduction to
Christian tantra as exemplified in Jesus and Mary Magdalene.

Luke, Helen. *Old Age.* New York: Parabola Books, 1987. A luminous
and wise guide to the emergence of wisdom and wholeness in the
human person during the final years of life. While this book is not
specifically theological in its objectives, it presents an extraordinary
portrait of the kenotic path lived to its completion.

Marion, Jim. *Putting on the Mind of Christ: The Inner Work of Christian Spirituality.* Charlottesville, Va.: Hampton Roads, 2000. An
engaging and highly original study of Jesus as a master of the transformation of consciousness.

Mayers, Gregory. *Listening to the Desert: Secrets of Spiritual Maturity
from the Desert Fathers and Mothers.* Liguori, Mo.: Liguori/Tri-
umph, 1996. The desert tradition considered from the perspective
of spiritual transformation.

Needleman, Jacob. *Lost Christianity.* Garden City, N.Y.: Doubleday,
1980. Reprint, Boston: Element Books, 1993. The original and still
classic study of the lost wisdom tradition within Christianity.

Nicoll, Maurice. *The New Man.* 1950. Reprint, Boulder, Colo.:
Shambhala, 1981. An interpretation of key parables and teachings
in the New Testament from a wisdom perspective. Nicoll was a
first-generation student of G. I. Gurdjieff as well as a student of
Carl Jung.

Pagels, Elaine. *Beyond Belief.* New York: Vintage Books, 2004. A highly accessible and compelling study of early Christianity's movement
from an experience-based religion *of* Jesus to a belief-based religion
about Jesus.

——. *The Gnostic Gospels.* New York: Vintage Books, 1981. The first
popular study of the Nag Hammadi codex and Christianity's sup-
pressed wisdom teachings.

Palmer, Martin. *The Jesus Sutras: Rediscovering the Lost Scrolls of Taoist
Christianity.* New York: Ballantine, 2001. A new discovery of a heretofore unknown strand of Christianity that traveled from its Near

Eastern homeland all the way across Central Asia and intertwined with the traditional oriental streams of *sophia perennis*.

Panikkar, Raimon. *Christophany: The Fullness of Man.* Maryknoll, N.Y.: Orbis Books, 2004. A dense but incomparably brilliant and compelling study of the Wisdom Jesus in a universal mystical context.

The Rule of St. Benedict. Collegeville, Minn.: Liturgical Press, 1980. A sumptuous anniversary edition of the St. Benedict's classic rule for his "school for the Lord's service," including Latin and English versions side by side and extensive notes and commentaries.

Scott, Bernard Brandon. *Hear Then the Parable.* Minneapolis, Minn.: Fortress Press, 1989. A comprehensive study of paradox and reversal in the parables of Jesus by a distinguished New Testament scholar.

Shapiro, Rami. *The Divine Feminine in Biblical Wisdom Literature.* Woodstock, Vt.: SkyLight Paths, 2005. A highly accessible introduction to the core texts of Jewish wisdom, the immediate nurturing ground for Jesus's own wisdom teaching.

Sherrard, Philip. *Christianity: Lineaments of a Sacred Tradition.* Brookline, Mass.: Holy Cross Orthodox Press, 1998. An articulate and compelling re-visioning of Christianity's wisdom heritage by a contemporary Orthodox scholar.

Smith, Andrew Philip. *The Lost Sayings of Jesus.* Woodstock, Vt.: SkyLight Paths, 2006. A fascinating kaleidoscope of "other takes" on Jesus from early Christianity's closest religious neighbors.

Smith, Huston. *Forgotten Truth: The Common Vision of the World's Religions.* San Francisco: HarperSanFrancisco, 1976. An illuminating exploration by one of the world's foremost scholars of comparative religion of the wisdom common ground underlying the great religious traditions of the world.

Smoley, Richard. *Inner Christianity: A Guide to the Esoteric Tradition.* Boston, Mass.: Shambhala, 2002. A clear and helpful introduction to the Christian inner tradition, including theology and metaphysics, history, and spiritual practice.

Tomberg, Valentin [published anonymously]. *Meditations on the Tarot: A Journey into Christian Hermeticism.* Translated by Robert Powell. New York: Tarcher/Putnam, 2002. This magisterial study is a profound synthesis of Christian mystical and esoteric wisdom. Tomberg traveled the route of classic hermeticism (sacred magic and alchemy) and anthroposophy before his conversion to Roman Catholicism during the 1940s, which altered the course of his life's work. While the book is dense and often frustratingly categorical in its assertions, its understanding of the symbolic and mystical implications of Christian dogma is simply unparalleled.

Versluis, Arthur. *Wisdom's Children: A Christian Esoteric Tradition.* Albany: State University of New York Press, 2000. This history of the spiritual descendents of Jacob Boehme is also a comprehensive study of the theory and practice of wisdom, including a remarkable chapter on the science of the imagination.

Ward, Benedicta, ed. *The Sayings of the Desert Fathers: The Alphabetical Collection.* Kalamazoo, Mich.: Cistercian, 1984. The classic source-book for the sayings and teachings of the Desert Fathers and Mothers, with an insightful introduction to the wisdom dimension of their spiritual practice.

Wilber, Ken. *The Eye of the Spirit: An Integral Vision for a World Gone Slightly Mad.* Boston, Mass.: Shambhala, 1997. Of Wilber's prolific writings, this volume contains his most concentrated introduction to the "perennial philosophy."

———. *Integral Spirituality.* Boston, Mass.: Shambhala, 2006. A highly readable and accessible introduction to Wilber's "integral" paradigm, with important new tools for clarifying metaphysical muddles and heading off religious tunnel vision. A foundational textbook for interspiritual wisdom studies.

Index

By Cynthia Bourgeault from Shambhala

Chanting the Psalms

A practical guide to the Christian practice of psalmody—chanting the biblical book of Psalms—that anyone can use to make this practice a part of their life. You don't need to be musical or a monk to do it. The book comes with an instructive audio CD in which Cynthia and friends teach simple techniques and melodies anyone can learn.